"*Monetary theory is like a Japanese garden. It has aesthetic unity born of variety; an apparent simplicity that conceals a sophisticated reality; a surface view that dissolves in ever deeper perspectives. Both can be fully appreciated only if examined from many different angles, only if studied leisurely but in depth. Both have elements that can be enjoyed independently of the whole, yet attain their full realization only as part of the whole*"

Milton Friedman, "The Optimum Quantity of Money"

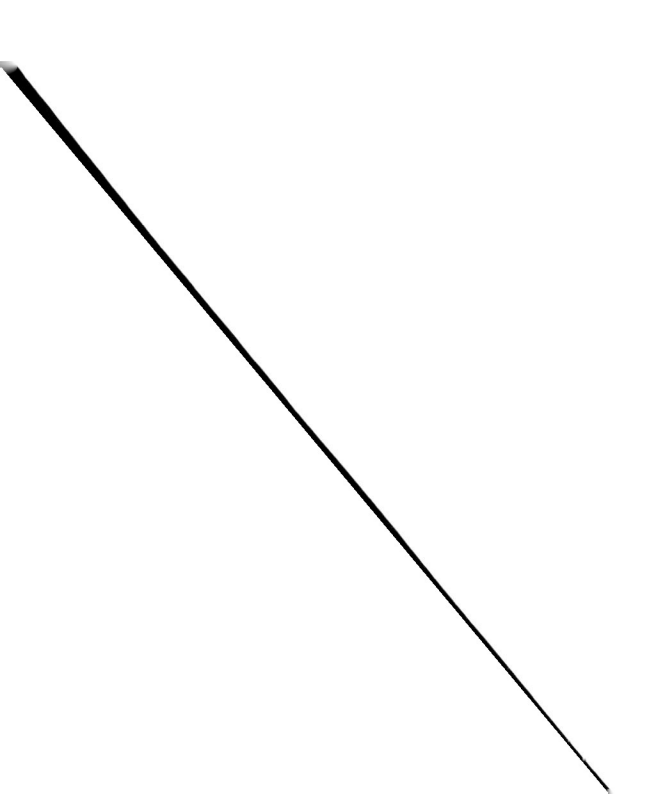

For love of money

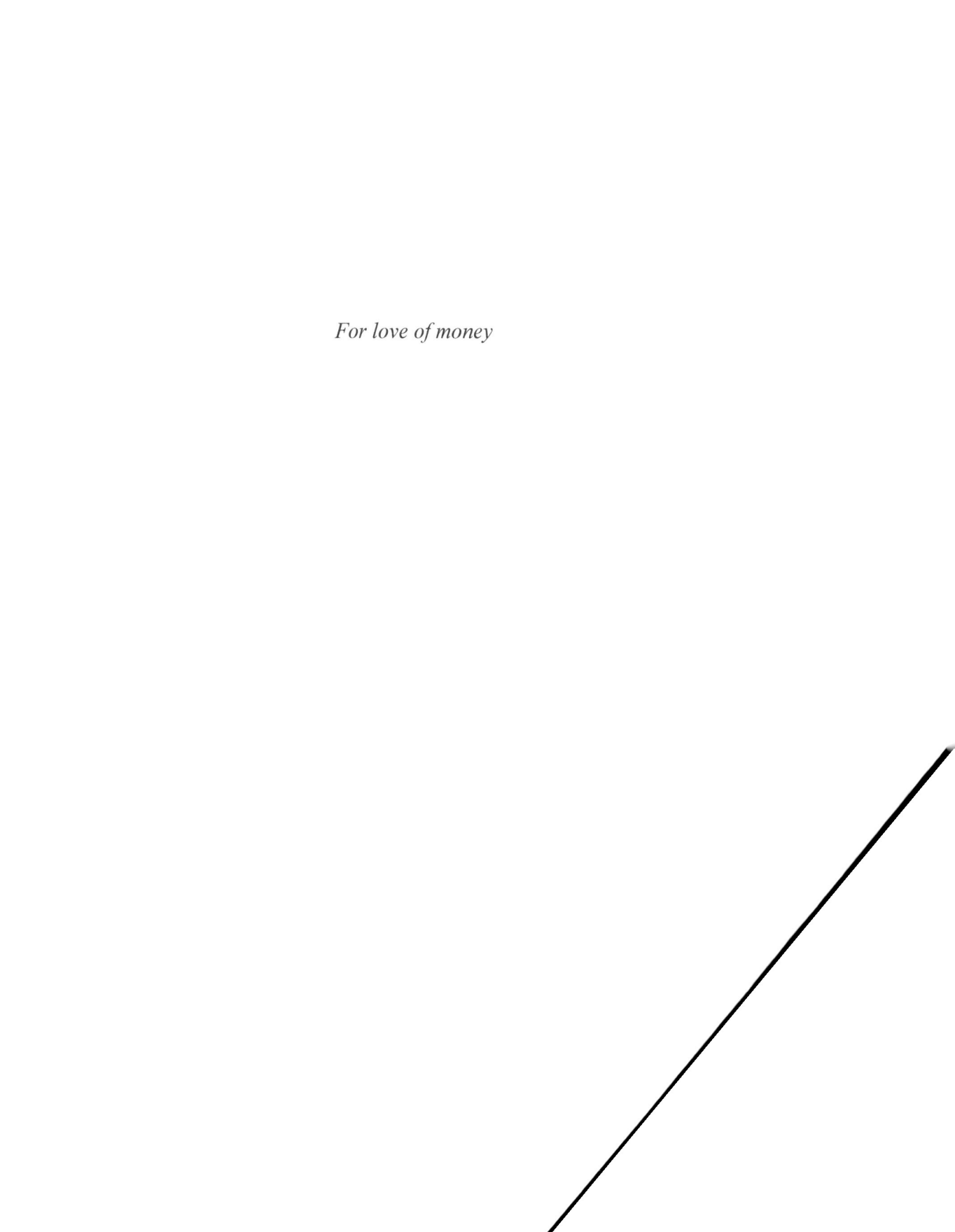

FRED J. SMITH

NICOLA PENCHEV

QUANTUM MONEY

A WEB-BASED SYSTEM OF MONEY AND CREDIT

The actual algorithms implementing the concepts of the book are protected by patents filed with the US Patent and Trademark Office. Licenses for the public sector for non-commercial use can be made available free of charge.

The authors can be contacted at:

n.p.penchev@gmail.com

fred.jos.smith@gmail.com

ISBN-13: 978-1517264048

ACKNOWLEGMENTS

The book builds on the work of E.C. Riegel on producer-issued credit ("The Valun System") and separation of money from the state; the work of Silvio Gesell on demurrage-charged currencies; F.A. Hayek's work on denationalization of money and competition between currencies; the "social credit" philosophy of C.H. Douglas, the "time dollars" of Edgar Cahn, the "public bank" solution of Ellen Brown, the "Chicago Plan" for banking reform, and the classics of the Austrian and Chicago schools on money, banking and credit.

Much inspiration and valuable insights come from the works of Andrew Jackson, Ben Dyson, C.A.E. Goodhart, Frederick Soddy, George A. Selgin, James Rickards, Jerome F. Smith, Lewis D. Solomon, Margrit Kennedy, Mark Novus, Melanie Swan, Michael Rowbotham, Paul Grignon, Ray Dalio, Richard Douthwaite, Robert Guttman, Steven Johnson and a list of excellent authors on money, credit, monetary reform, information technology, networks and complexity theory too long to be included in this introduction.

Most of the system's logic and components are previously described in various works authored/co-authored by Bernard Lietaer and Thomas Greco.

The software technology is borrowed from the existing digital currencies – the "blockchain". The collective intelligence philosophy behind platforms such as Wikipedia and the PageRank search algorithm is applied to power the IT-based Hayekian currency discovery process.

References of the work of the above-mentioned authors do not imply their endorsement for the book in any way.

TABLE OF CONTENTS

FOREWORD

THERE WAS NO INTERNET

➢ when, millennia ago, primitive men first engaged in *barter*, overcoming the limitations of self-sufficiency;

➢ when, millennia ago, precious metals took the center stage as *media of exchange*, overcoming the limitations of barter;

➢ when, centuries ago, Italian goldsmiths started issuing gold warehousing receipts in excess of their existing gold reserves, thus inventing *credit* and overcoming the limitations of prior gold accumulation for the development of free enterprise;

➢ when, during the last century, Lugwig von Mises wrote his classic "Theory of Money and Credit" laying the foundations of the libertarian understanding of money and banking; when E.C. Riegel wrote "The New Approach to Freedom" reclaiming from the state, on behalf of the people, the right to money issue; when Friedrich von Hayek argued for denationalization and choice in currency as the best guarantees for the long-run stability of the money system; and when Milton Friedman declared money "too important to be left to central bankers"...

AND THEN THE INTERNET ARRIVED. And the Internet changes everything. What if algorithms could be made to work with respect to the money system, and what effect would this have on the economic, environmental and societal challenges that we face? What if society's money system could be created via the voluntary interactions of millions of participants - by the invisible hand of collective intelligence – as opposed to the current centralized, top-down, bank-centric approach? Will individual actors – acting collectively via IT – achieve a better outcome for monetary management than the Mario Draghis and the Janet Yellens of this world? Will the spontaneous order arising out of individualism provide results superior to the centrally-planned status-quo? What if we approach the money system as a complex adaptive system and via IT implement in practice ideas trodden in the minds of scholars such as Friedrich Hayek, Milton Friedman, Irving Fisher and Edwin Riegel? Ideas long considered purely hypothetical, impossible to implement, mere thought experiments? Allowing us, in these times of economic uncertainty, to seek sound money and economic stability not back into the fetters of the gold standard, but instead full forward into the Information Age? Where code and information reign supreme, including the field of monetary policy and finance? What if we could get code to do the monetary function of gold, and much more? What if the Bitcoin only barely lifted the curtain of "cyberspace monetarism"? What treasures for money and economics might be hidden out there in cyberspace? Could a collectively intelligent money system – an Information Age money system – disintermediate the current top-down, centrally managed, Industrial Age money system?

This book is a journey into the strange monetary realm that exists at the intersection between IT and monetarism - a journey full of economic miracles and bizarre economic phenomena – a wonderland of economies operating constantly at full employment, economies in which concepts such as "Keynesian interventions", "QE", "exchange rates", "depressions", "base money", "government social programs", "Philips curve" - and many more - are simply *not defined*; economies in which access to basic education, basic healthcare, and to economic participation are natural rights for each and every individual, economies in which money comes into existence and flows without the intermediation of the state, or the commercial banks.

A wonderland which - technologically at least – is perfectly within our reach.

THE CURRENT SYSTEM OF MONEY AND CREDIT

"Money is merely a human construct…that was designed in and for another age"

Bernard Lietaer, **Jacqui Dunne**, *"Rethinking Money"*

WHAT IS MONEY, AND THE QUEST FOR SOUND MONEY

"The analogy between the need for invariant units of length and weight and the need for an invariant unit of value is appealing...to be serviceable, units of length, weight, and value must be invariant over time."
Roger Garrison, "The Costs of a Gold Standard"

What is money – medium of exchange, unit of account, store of value

Living all alone on his island, Robinson Crusoe never needed any money – a pile of gold would probably have had absolutely no practical use, a pile of paper with ink on it (banknotes) – well may be he could start a fire with it, just as he would with any other piece of paper. Being self-sufficient, he never owed anything to anybody, and vice versa. He never exchanged anything with anyone. He never had to measure via some unit the value of his goods *vis-à-vis* other people's goods, and hence didn't need that (hypothetical in his case) measure to be stable through time.

Money is *social*. It arises only when there is division of labor, hence a need for exchange. Direct exchange however (the so called barter) whether on an explicit *quid-pro-quo* basis or as communal gifts and favors (in smaller communities), is so hard to execute – to exchange, say, an investment fund's money management services for pizzas at Papa Joey's Pizza, would be hard if not impossible...It might work once – to reciprocate a hot stock tip for a hot pizza, let's say, but a universally accepted medium of exchange would have made things much easier – the fund managers provide hot advice to limited partners for that media, and then Papa Joey provides the hot pizzas – again for the same media. The process of indirect exchange requires ability to measure the value changing hands (how many of Papa Joey's pizzas for how many hours of the fund managements' advisory services), and that measure has to hold steady through time – to avoid disappointment and to keep the fund managers and Papa Joey motivated to provide those advisory services and hot pizzas.

> **Money is an agreement, within a community, to use *something* standardized as a medium of exchange[1].**

That *something* could be *anything*, as long as the community agrees to use it as exchange media. It could grow – slowly on Mondays and faster on Sundays, it could go left at first and then green, it could have babies, grow leaves, it could have a pleasant sound, smell, and great appearance. It could have a geographic, national dimension. A temporal one. Or it could be poetic. Warm and kind, elegant, beautiful. Or it could be competitive. Fiercely so. Or joyful. Paranoid. Vicious. It could have physical carrier – one or many. It might be capable of inflicting pain even – who knows??

> **Money could be *anything*.**

As long as the community agrees that this is what its *money* is – so be it. Money is a mind game of the community.

Whatever money is, it is important that it does a good job measuring value – If you can't measure it, you can't manage it. How many chicken for a cow, for a kilo of sugar, for a liter of wine. Money needs ***units***.

And then, the values measured in those units using that medium, must hold steady through time. If today I agree to sell my cow for some number of money units, knowing that these units could get me, say, 18 chicken today if I needed chicken, I want next week, when I do need the chicken, to be able to get them – all 18 of them. If, for some reason, the chicken salesman says then that my money has rotten since I've sold the cow last week, and is willing to sell only 10 chicken for my (already rotten) cow money, I would be very disappointed with this money. Just why did I have to bring that cow to the market in the first place!! Money has to be a reliable ***store of value*** in order to encourage exchange to take place.

---

[1] Bernard Lietaer, Jacqui Dunne "Rethinking Money"

Why money – breaking the shackles of self-sufficiency and barter

The first major breakthrough in monetary innovation was the acceptance of a medium of exchange that separated the act of providing wealth to society from the act of claiming wealth from society – the double coincidence of wants that barter required – coincidence in terms of (1) the types of goods to be exchanged, (2) the amounts in which they are needed by the two parties, and (3) the time and place of the exchange. By avoiding the huge transaction costs of barter, money greatly facilitated the exchange process, hence the wealth creation.

In the reciprocal-gift-exchange communities, money eliminated the memory lapses on behalf of some of the lazier gift recipients (memory lapses always on the side of omitting gifts owed to others, aka "credit risk"), removing the option of free loading, forcing everyone into just contribution to the welfare of the community.

Thus, millennia ago, people arrived *ad hoc* to the agreement that precious metals will be money – medium of exchange, unit of account, store of value. Those who were good at producing something could specialize in it, produce more than they could consume, and provide the excess to society on a *quid-pro-quo* basis through the money system. The cowgirl could raise as many cows as she could, without worrying if the chickenman will be there with the right number of chicken, at the right time, and in need of a cow – there was *money* to smooth the exchange process. The economy became a *network*.

The Invisible Hand could begin working its miracles.

Why money matters, a lot

"..an improperly managed money supply leads to much greater economic discoordination than an incorrect supply of any other good or service. Excess demand or excess supply of money affects spending in numerous other markets, and hence affects the entire system of market price and profit signals. One can think of the market as being like a wheel, with money as the hub, prices as the spokes, and other goods as the rim. A change in the relation of one good to the rest is like a tightening or loosening of a single spoke: it has a great effect on one small part of the wheel, but much less effect on the rest of the wheel. A change in the relation of money to other goods is like moving the hub: it has a great effect on all parts of the wheel, because it moves all spokes at once. Adjust a spoke – a particular price – improperly, and you make one small part of the wheel wobble; adjust the hub – money – improperly, and you bend the whole wheel out of shape.

The far-reaching consequences of monetary disequilibrium are a matter of grave concern precisely because the market prices have a coordinating role to perform. Incorrect adjustments in the money supply promote *general* calculational chaos. They undermine the normal, beneficial operation of the price system in guiding entrepreneurial action. If the money industry does not function well, then the rest of the economic system cannot function well. "

George A. Selgin "The Theory of Free Banking"

The money unit and the money system

For a period in the past, cattle were used as money. In this case the money unit requires feeding, watering, it reproduces, and may also provide milk. The money system that would have developed would involve (initially at least) farmers as "bankers" and cattle farms as "banks".

A very different money system would be one using a commodity – some metal for example – as a money unit. Smelters, goldsmiths (initially at least) would be bankers, and amounts of metal (gold) – money units.

Each money unit brings about a peculiar money system, with its own peculiar features.

Money systems obey the Metcalfe's law: the more users adopt a particular money system – the more useful it becomes for existing and new users. A money system is thus a natural monopoly – it is cheaper for one system to provide all the benefits, as opposed to having many money systems competing simultaneously with each other.

What is a monetary system

The set of rules – explicit (laws, regulations), and implicit (assumed by default, conventions) – determining what money is, how it comes into being, how it ends, how it moves around and how fast.

A monetary system must first determine *what is used as money* – stones, skins, commodities, information, etc. – whatever works best for the community.

A monetary system must determine the *optimum quantity of money* in circulation. According to various researchers, currently 97% of all money is created by the commercial banks – they issue to borrowers newly created media (credit) and keep a record of what the borrowers must repay – at which point (at repayment of the loan) the newly issued credit is destroyed. The commercial banks charge something for themselves in the process – the so called "interest", plus maybe some operating fees. The central bank, by determining the level of the interest rate in the economy (and with some other tools), tries to encourage/discourage borrowing so as to control the money stock in the economy and to prevent inflation/deflation. *Money should be available within the economy – not too much and not too little.*

A monetary system must determine the *velocity of money* into circulation. Money shouldn't overheat the economy (possibly causing inflation, bubbles, too many imports, etc.), or freeze it (due to hoarding of money and lack of lending). *Money should move around – not too fast, not too slow.*

A monetary system must provide an *anchor for the store of value function*. Money should hold its value, or all hell breaks loose. Fluctuations in the value of money hurt the exchange process – the very *reason-d'étre* for the existence of money – inflation hurts lenders and stops incentives to sell (better not sell now, prices will soon rise, hold on to real wealth), deflation hurts borrowers, and stops incentives to buy (better not buy now, prices will soon fall, hold on to your money). Therefore, money should be a reliable and predictable measuring rod for wealth transfers across time and across economic actors within the economy. The gold standard was used for many years for this function. Currently, it is people, mostly at central banks, who try to ensure the soundness of money through their (possibly politically influenced) policies. *Money should hold fast over time.*

A monetary system must provide a reliable and safe *payment system*. The payment system shouldn't be held hostage to outside risks, such as financial system risks – credit risks, liquidity risks, etc. *Money should be able to move around safely.*

Typical *monetary institutions* are parliaments, central banks and commercial banks.

What is a financial system

The set of rules of what you do with your (or other people's) money: how you earn it, how you protect it from various risks, how you multiply it, how you transfer it – across time, across actors within the economy.

A financial system seeks to find the answer how much an asset costs, as part of a process of efficient capital allocation – there is an *asset price discovery mechanism*

A financial system facilitates investment, *transforming shorter-term maturities into longer-term capital.*

A financial system deals with *transfer and pricing of various risks.*

Typical *financial institutions* are the commercial and investment banks, the insurance companies, the various investment funds, the stock exchanges, the commodity exchanges, etc.

THE EVOLUTION OF THE MONEY UNIT

Shells, skins, stones, paper, cattle, copper, silver, gold – the list of *things* used as money is long. Gold stuck with humans as a money unit the longest. Why?

Why gold (and not copper, or diamonds, or whatever)

- Gold is scarce. It is not widely available in nature, and is not easy to mine and process.
- Gold is durable. Golden teeth found in the Egyptian pyramids can be used today. Gold found in ship wrecks on the bottom of the ocean is still nice and shiny underneath all that sand.
- Gold looks good. It is nice and shiny and yellow, doesn't rust on you and taint your clothes. It can be put on your ears, on your chest, on your wrist – and you'll look good with it.
- It is easily divisible (unlike diamonds), it is easy to mold, it cannot be easily broken or crushed.
- It comes in only one variety; it is very dense, and hence counterfeits can be easily detected.
- It doesn't get used up in industrial applications (relatively few exist).
- Gold is transnational, independent of governments.
- A small amount of gold can cover a large economic transaction – as compared to silver or copper, for example.
- In times of crisis – physical gold is nobody's liability and can be trusted (no counterparty risk), and also cannot be printed at will.

How did the gold coin evolve into a "gold standard"

Through fractional reserve banking. The "reserves" of gold in the goldsmiths' vaults determined how much gold warehousing receipts /money/ the goldsmith could issue against interest[2].

The last version of the gold standard was created in 1944 when the leaders of the world got together in Bretton Woods, New Hampshire, to fix the international monetary system with the end of WWII. The US dollar was pegged to gold at $35/ounce, and all other currencies were pegged to the dollar. The Agreement also created the institutions required for its maintenance – the International Trade Organization (to avoid trade wars), and the IMF as a lender to governments and central banks to help keep their currencies pegged to gold. At the time of creation of the Bretton Woods agreement, the US had some 75% of the world's gold, large trade surpluses, and was the undisputed world economic leader. This was about to change, though, in the following decades.

Keynes, the leader of the British negotiators, insisted for a supranational global currency as a reserve asset. American monetary nationalism, however, prevailed, and the pegged-to-gold US dollar was established as the world reserve asset. This bestowed to the US the "exorbitant privilege" to print dollars to pay for imports, and then issue low-interest government debt to soak those dollars back. This meant the currency – the US dollar – was never presented to claim real output, real goods and services from the US economy. The result was profligacy, both as a government policy and personal consumption of the American consumers.

Why the gold standard worked (for a while)

The gold standard worked best in the years preceding WWI. At that time it was a decentralized, multipolar system, not depending on any single stabilizing dominant power. The main reasons for its success were the commitment and cooperation of central banks and governments, which established the credibility of the standard. Should any country run low on gold, private funds would flow in its direction *in anticipation* of the central banks' actions, so little intervention was even necessary.

---

[2]A brief overview of banking is provided in chapter "The Evolution of the Money System"

Why the gold standard stopped working (eventually)

President Nixon was forced to finally end the gold standard in 1971 because the US banks were creating dollars via fractional reserve banking, those dollars ended up overseas via American imports and American investment abroad, and as foreign governments began redeeming dollars for gold, the US began to run out of reserves. So the gold standard had to end. The world went fiat. The value of a nation's currency was to be determined by "philosopher kings" in charge of central banks and treasury departments.

Main weakness of the gold standard

Exogenous money supply shocks are possible – via new gold discoveries or mining technology improvements.

Shortage of monetary gold under a gold standard can constrain commerce.

Gold as an automatic international adjustment mechanism is too bitter of a medicine. Economists call this "recessionary bias" – a country running low on gold must raise interest rate to stem the outflow, to increase savings and reduce demand for imports; painful restrictive fiscal and monetary policies are required. Whereas, absent a gold standard, a central bank and an accommodating government can ease the pain of economic slowdowns, at least in the short run.

A gold standard also transmits destabilizing impulses from one country to another. As one country takes steps to defend its gold stocks via increase in interest rates, other countries must retaliate with similar measures.

The illusion of "gold-backed" currency

"A currency backed by gold" is a misnomer. A currency can only be backed by the goods and services of its issuer. With that dollar bill in your pocket you need to buy pizzas and haircuts – not gold – just ask King Midas about it. Only a gold miner, a gold processor or a gold retailer/trader could issue a currency "backed by gold". A much better definition of a gold-pegged national currency would be something like "issue-constrained by the amount of gold available with issuer". A nation's currency can only be backed by the productive capacity of that nation. The real wealth of nations is the total output of the goods and services of the economy. Gold is only a carrier of a stable measure.

A currency "backed by the full faith and credit of the US government" is a misnomer, too. A much better definition of a fiat dollar would be "backed by the collective output of the US economy, and not restrained in its issue by a commodity anchor, or by any other automatic mechanism".

Conspiracy theories concerning gold

Western governments and central banks have sold most of their gold, or leased it to bullion banks, etc. (who in turn sold it) and in effect cannot come up with the physical metal, at least not immediately.

Gold is manipulated by Western central banks on COMEX in the US and LBMA in London, where naked short positions (with cash settlement only) are possible. This is done because a high price of gold is usually interpreted as lack of confidence in the dollar. At crucial times, there is prevention of the signaling effect of gold – the crisis barometer of gold is not allowed to sound an alarm. The newly opened Shanghai Gold Exchange does not allow such a speculative trade – you must own the metal to be able to sell it.

China, Russia and India accumulate gold, and take steps towards the introduction of a gold-backed currency to replace the dollar in international trade and investment. The BRICS bank, and the recently opened gold exchange in Shanghai, are steps in this direction.

Essence of the gold standard and key benefits

"Compared, however, with the various schemes for monetary management on a national scale, the gold standard had three very important advantages: it created in effect an international currency without submitting national monetary policy to the decisions of an international authority; it made monetary policy in a great measure automatic and thereby predictable; and the changes in the supply of basic money which its mechanism secured were on the whole in the right direction" **Friedrich Hayek** "Individualism and Economic Order"

Under a true gold standard the various currencies are just different names for weights of gold. The paper (bank) notes are redeemable in actual gold. The gold standard protects the users of a currency from abuse by the person in charge of the printing press – you can't print gold. As such, a gold standard is key to protection of private property rights of citizens *vis-à-vis* governments.

Domestically, through the price stability it implies, a gold standard encourages saving and investment. Internationally, a gold standard encourages foreign trade and investment by eliminating forex risk.

In international trade and investment, a gold standard is an automatic rebalancing mechanism between countries – if country A experiences high growth and hence draws in capital from a slow-growing country B, interest rates in country B go up to stem the outflow of gold, this causes further economic slowdown and reduction in wages in country B. Thus country B now has greater incentives for savings and capital creation (higher interest rate), greater incentive to attract capital (higher interest rate and lower wages), hence a basis for a healthy recovery. The processes in country B are sometimes referred to as "creative destruction", absolutely necessary for the constant renewal of a capitalist economy.

The main function achieved via gold was stability of the purchasing power of money within the money system (ensure the store of value function of money).

Gold is not some God-given center of the money Universe, however. The strange pagan ritual of digging yellow metal out in South Africa and Siberia to re-bury it again underground in New York and London, amidst all that medieval air of mystery, secrecy and mystique – it went with the money unit and the money system of the time. And times change.

In the words of Hayek "A wisely and impartially controlled system of managed currency for the whole world might, indeed, be superior to it (the gold standard) in all its aspects. But this is not a practical proposition for a long while yet".

This was said back in the 70's though. A lot of propositions not practical back then are quite practical today. Like carrying your telephone around in your hand, or taking a picture with it; or carrying your color TV set around; cars without drivers; coin mining within a group of interconnected machines (Bitcoin).....or algorithms that can keep the value of an electronic currency constant, or measure the reliability of its issuer.

"Who needs gold when we have Alan Greenspan?" was a title in the financial press from the not too distant past. Several years went by, the 2007-2008 debacle took place, and amidst all that money printing, the outcry seems to be "Who needs Ben Bernanke, bring back the gold!".

"Who needs gold when we have the Silicon Valley?" is the future-oriented proposal of this book. The nostalgia over gold is misplaced: gold was a local maximum, a temporary repose in the evolution of money – a **host** for the money system. A good host, reliable and solid (not too bright, though). But now we have another potential host, a much smarter host – the Internet. And on the Internet, money systems of every shape, form and variety are possible. We just have to pick the one we like.

"The belief persists to this day that money, to be sound, must promise the delivery of gold or silver. The essential quality of money, however, is the promise to deliver value in any commodity at the choice of the holder". **E.C. Riegel**, "The new approach to freedom"

The evolution of the money unit: summary

Through trial and error, human societies – in the process of barter exchanges and reciprocal gift exchanges – came up with the social technology of money: medium of exchange, store of value and unit of account. For millennia, gold was money – it was scarce, shiny, solid. With the introduction of fractional reserve banking, it evolved into a pivot for the money system, assuring the stability of money as a store of value.

What money became after the end of the gold standard in 1971 was merely the idea that the value of the currency unit of a country was the total wealth of the country divided by the outstanding currency units. Thus, the money unit became a simple data structure, consisting of essentially two main fields – "value" and "issuer[3]". The "value" field can contain any positive number with up to two decimal points; the whole numbers can have paper (25% linen and 75% cotton) as a physical carrier – aka "bills" with "value" of 1, 2, 5, etc.; the decimal fractions can have metal carriers, colloquially referred to as "coins". If in the field "issuer" we fill "US Federal Reserve" for example, the money unit would carry a unique sign that looks like that: "$", and the money unit would be colloquially referred to as a "dollar" ['dä-lər]. A more precise definition of the money unit currently in use globally would be "a two-field data structure, with the option of a physical carrier" – that's all the dollar/pound/yen/etc. are. The term "paper money" is no more meaningful than the term "paper poetry" - paper just happens to be the carrier of the value-claiming information; genuine paper money would mean value is measured in some paper-quantifying metric – a kilo of paper, a square centimeter of paper, something like that. And then people would store their precious paper in a vault, and get warehousing receipts as evidence of their, well, paper-wealth, etc., etc. – the whole gig as under the gold scenario... Well it's obviously not the case – it's not the paper, it's *what's written* on the paper – the information – that counts. Paper is the chaff, information is the wheat. "Paper money" looks like paper money, feels like paper money – but it isn't. It is information money. "Paper money" (or "Money for paper", or "Money on paper") is just the same as "Windows for Desktop", or "Windows on a Desktop" – information on a carrier.

Gold was information money, too. Only we rarely saw it this way, blinded by all that glitter and millennia of groupthink. What those goldsmiths back in the 13th century stored was essentially information – information about how much real wealth the gold owners could claim from society. Information (reliably stored and carried) as gold, disguised as gold, and universally accepted in its golden disguise via a very strong network effect.

That cowgirl 3000 years ago, bringing her cow to the market and not in immediate need of any equally valuable good or service, needed a proof, a ledger entry, a record with Mr. Market, with that proverbial Walrasian auctioneer – a record recognizable by everyone out there in the community, a record stable through time – about the fact that she did provide her cow (the "quid") on a *quid-pro-quo* basis to the community. And she needed – eventually, when she indeed decided to claim her entitlement to equivalent amount of goods and services from the community (the "quo") – to be able to do so using that record. But how do you make such a stable, widely accepted record 3000 years ago? Gold turned out to be the best available proxy. But that was 3000 years ago, when people played Farmville in real life.

Money has been information from Day One – information about a *quid-pro-quo* exchange, about transfer of value across economic actors and across time – and the idea that money can be anything else *but* information is only a "stubbornly persisting illusion[4]".We've been blinded all along by the information carriers. All those carriers were only intermediate steps, local maxima, in the search of *money* for its true host – the Intel chip.

As to why in the Information Age we don't use a money unit richer in useful information attributes – a multidimensional, complex data structure with richer data fields about the exchange (as opposed to the current two-field structure) – well, this will remain as one of those deep mysteries of the early 21st century, not subject to rational explanation[5].

---

[3]In reality, several other minor information fields exist on the Federal Reserve note
[4]The term used by Albert Einstein with respect to time
[5]"Network effect", "natural monopoly of the money system", "lock-in effect" might be some of the right answers.

THE EVOLUTION OF THE MONEY SYSTEM

"Banking – it's a process that even today, few bankers understand"
Milton Friedman

Why banking as organization of money – breaking the shackles of prior liquidity accumulation

Centuries ago, members of society, using commodities (mostly gold) as money, managed to self-organize themselves into economic activities of their choice to produce goods and services to the best of their capabilities – within the safety net of money-intermediated exchange environment.

But what if you had a great idea for a good or a service, willingness to work hard for it – and no gold? Great ideas don't always come only to those with the gold, you know.

Faced with a lack of formal venues within the existing money system to fund great ideas, entrepreneurs whose vision outstripped their available resources, resorted to *fraud* (entrepreneurs have always been an ingenious bunch, for better or worse). They *cheated* the system, as it existed back then. Original sin – *fraud* – gave rise to the next great invention in monetarism – credit – the ability to claim goods and services from society without having first accumulated the purchasing power to do so[6].

In order to channel resources from society for the execution of their vision, entrepreneurs, facing resource constraints, *pretended* they had prior accumulated liquidity – with a little help from their friendly local neighborhood goldsmith. Here is how it happened:

around 13th century, Venice, Italy

Dennis, the local goldsmith, was having a drink at the pub after a long day of work. His business was doing well – he made gold jewelry, weighed and measured the fineness of gold coins for his customers, accepted gold for safekeeping in his vault, issued gold warehousing receipts. Dennis was a third generation goldsmith, from a well-known and well-respected family; now in his 50's, he was solid, well-connected and well-established – "pillar of the community" – and his gold warehousing receipts were as good as the gold itself; for convenience, in daily shopping people would even exchange the receipts instead of the gold, safe in the knowledge that their gold was intact in Dennis' vault; customers would even ask, upon depositing their gold with him, to be given not one receipt for the whole amount deposited, but instead several bearer receipts for smaller amounts, specifically for the purpose of facilitating the use of Dennis' gold warehousing receipts in the course of their daily shopping.

As he was drinking his wine, his cousin Vinny walked in. Vinny was the complete opposite of Dennis – still in his thirties, he liked to have good time, had a quick eye for pretty girls – and spent all his money chasing them. Money came easy to Vinny, he always came up with *something* to earn some extra gold. Too bad for him, because his money, although easy to come, were even easier to go.

This time Vinny looked distraught. "He's out of gold again" thought Dennis. "I wonder what he's up to this time."

"Dennis! Dennis! Oh, life is so unfair!! You won't believe the golden opportunity I came across this time" Vinny looked around the pub to make sure no one was eavesdropping and lowered his voice to a whisper. "Salt. Lots of it. Just arrived in Genoa, a whole ship. And there are no buyers! And you know what – that ship must leave in a few days. They are thinking of dumping all the salt in the ocean as no one would keep it on the port for free!". All of a sudden, Dennis was all ears. He knew the local butchers were out of salt, and were offering gold - lots of it – for salt. Vinny continued "The local butchers – they will *kill* for a bag of salt. Their meat stocks are beginning to rot. I could make a killing!" And after a deep sigh, he continued. "Life is so unfair, though. Just as I can finally strike it rich, I am absolutely out of money! I need to buy supplies for the trip, pay the horse carriages, pay the salt to the shipping company – some 60 ounces of gold in total. And the butchers will pay me 120 for sure once I return with

---

[6]The (artificial, convoluted, confusing) explanation given to kids and academics is that goldsmiths' reserves were "lent out".
Yeah right…. For this – face saving - explanation refer to "The meaning of money" by Hartley Withers.

12

the salt! I tried to offer my IOUs for the trip supplies, for the horse carriages, but no one would accept my IOUs! This is so unfair". He slumped in his seat, silent and heartbroken.

Dennis' mind raced. He knew Vinny was right – it *was* a golden opportunity. He knew the butchers – they've been in business for so long, they knew their trade, they were going to pay – top price! – for the salt. 60 ounces of net profit! For 10 days of work! This was unheard of. And all this money was going down the drain simply because no one would accept Vinny's IOUs!

Dennis looked around the pub, slowly leant over to Vinny and began whispering in his ear, deliberately and self-assuredly: "Now listen up, Vinny, and listen good...I'll help you get the salt, and we'll split the profit. Here is what we gonna do. I'll write you gold warehousing receipts for 60 ounces of gold – fake ones, but no one except you and me will know about it – don't worry, no one pries in my vault. I'll say you brought some gold with me today for safekeeping. With the fake receipts you will pay for the trip supplies, pay for the horse carriages, pay the shipping company for the salt, then you sell the salt to the butchers for 120 ounces. You come straight back to me with the money – we'll destroy 60 receipts to restore the balance between gold and warehousing receipts (to make up for the fake ones) – and keep 60 good ones. We split 30 for you and 30 for me – that's my interest in the deal. Just in case something goes wrong and in order to make sure you don't blow the money, I'll mortgage your house, and if I don't see my money, I'll sell the house to replenish my gold reserves with 60 ounces of gold to back up the fake receipts I issued you. And keep your big mouth shut!How do you like my deal?"Of course Vinny liked the deal. Free money! No need for gold! They shook hands, got up and went straight to Dennis' house. Dennis made the receipts for the non-existing gold, they filled out the mortgage deed for Vinny's house, and Vinny went to get the salt.

The End

_____

With their fast little trick, the cousins made monetary history. Let's stress-test the situation to see the true significance of their hush-hush deal:

Stress-test 1: Dennis drops dead.

Vinny, after leaving Dennis' house (the fake receipts tucked in his pocket), bought trip supplies right away, paid the horse carriages and left for Genoa. And then Dennis dropped dead. Absolutely, 100% dead.

The news of Dennis' unfortunate death spread quickly throughout Venice. The next day every one of his warehouse receipt holders lined up in front of his store to get their gold from the vault. Surprise, surprise! There were more receipts than there was gold! (the trip-supplies people didn't know their receipts had no gold to back them up, and no one knew there were any fake receipts to begin with). All hell broke loose. A sorcerer, also among the depositors, even tried to bring Dennis back from the dead, as obviously Dennis was the only one who could sort out the horrible mess with the missing gold and the extra receipts – but no luck. Dennis was still dead, and was still the only one who could solve the puzzle.

Stress-test conclusions: Dennis and Vinny's little trick fundamentally changed the essence of the gold warehousing receipts – *from claims on gold, claims as good as gold – they became claims on Dennis*, as obviously only Dennis could make good on all the claims. The claim-holders needed Dennis – alive and well – to handle the situation. The claims were now not as good as the gold they represented – they were only as good as Dennis' ability to come up with the gold. *They were Dennis' IOUs*. Dennis, *from a custodian, had become an investor*. The gold reserves in the vault were now only *a fraction* of the outstanding receipts. Eventually, this (essentially fraudulent, or at least initiated as fraudulent) activity became known as "*fractional reserve banking*"

Stress-test 2: Vinny drops dead.

Shortly after Vinny paid for the trip supplies, he dropped dead. Absolutely, 100% dead. This got Dennis very worried, because it meant the deal would not be concluded, and he would lose from his gold reserves the amount of the receipts he issued to Vinny which ended up in the trip supplies people. Dennis hurried to sell Vinny's house, but ever since Vinny's unfortunate death the citizens of Venice thought it was haunted by ghosts, and no one wanted to buy it, or at least no one wanted to buy it at a price anywhere near what Dennis needed to recover his losses. Dennis raised his clenched fist to the sky and yelled in anger "Vinny you schmuck! I gave you gold receipts as good as gold, and you gave me a promise you didn't keep! I knew your IOUs were no good. Rot in hell!".

Stress-test conclusions: Dennis exchanged his – trusted by the public, IOU (and we saw in stress-test 1 that it was essentially only an IOU) – for the IOU of Vinny (not trusted by the public), an IOU carrying "*credit risk*", and backed by collateral - in exchange for his expected "*interest*".

Stress-test 3: The horses drop dead.

Shortly after Vinny went on his trip, the horses dropped dead. This meant the deal could still be profitably executed, but on foot. This would take time. Eventually, Vinny would come back, receipts for 120 ounces of gold with him, but in the meantime Dennis' depositors expected their gold deposits to be accessible at any time, without delay. This eventually became known as "*maturity transformation*" – shorter-term deposits mismatched with longer-term investments.

Stress-test 4: Depositors nearly drop dead.

Somebody spread a rumor that Dennis gave gold to Vinny and Vinny blew it on booze and blondes, making bad deals and getting into the wrong brawls. Everybody received an anxiety attack and/or a heart attack, and ran to Dennis' store to get their gold from the unreliable goldsmith. This eventually became known as a "*run on the bank*".

Moreover, after depositors realized Dennis was no more the staid, safe pillar of the community he used to be for decades, but instead had become Dennis the Monetary Menace from Venice, the only way for Dennis to keep his customers was to lure them with a cut of the profits of his shady dealings with Vinny – not to say that other goldsmiths, seeing how profitable fake receipts issuance could be, also began *paying* depositors to have their gold instead of *getting paid* for safekeeping it. Dennis' receipts became "*interest-bearing deposits*".

Stress-test 5: The sorcerer props up the dead bodies.

As Dennis was raising in anger his clenched fist at the ghost of Vinny, the local sorcerer – Mr. Coleman Zacks – stopped by. As Dennis began to complain how he is stuck with dead Vinny's IOU, Mr. Coleman Zacks assured him he can help. First he propped Vinny's dead body, saying he wasn't exactly dead but more like undead, and then used his "securitization" magic and sold Vinny's IOU to unsuspecting investors. The way it worked was through moodies – little things living in his pocket, who were very moody. These moodies never saw any ghosts in Vinny or in Vinny's house during the good times, but in bad times they saw a ghost in every person and in every house. Mr. Coleman Zacks used the moodies to sing out loud that Vinny's IOU is good because his house was backing it up, there were no ghosts in it and never would be. There was, however, a price to pay for Dennis, as it always is with dark magic: having sold his soul for money, Dennis turned into a zombie himself; his previously reputable custodian business into a "*zombie bank*" – a custodian of dead customers' IOUs.

Now let us continue our story in a somewhat brighter mood. Let's assume no one died, no one got scared, and no one turned into a zombie. Vinny successfully sold the salt, and everybody was happy. Dennis realized he could make so much money this way – issuing fake receipts to Vinny (and others like Vinny who had bright ideas and good collateral but no gold). He only had to make sure he always had enough gold in the vault to redeem the occasional note holder who would ask her gold back, so no one would doubt his integrity or the safety of the gold deposited in his vault. This meant some 10% gold of the total amount of outstanding receipts had to be kept at any time in the vault, as a running gold balance.

Time went by. Other goldsmiths got in the gig as well. With so much money, trade flourished. Receipts issued in Venice started circulating in Genoa, and vice versa. Goldsmiths expanded geographically within a relatively short (manageable without advanced information technology) range. Goldsmiths started opening accounts with each other, so as to be able to easily honor each other's receipts.

As goldsmiths began to shuffle gold and receipts back and forth between themselves in settlement of trade receivables, the couriers would meet halfway between the goldsmiths' offices and sort through all the receipts and settle on a net basis. Goldsmiths realized it would be much easier if they had a structured clearing house, in which each goldsmith would keep some gold, and the clearing house would settle payments on a net basis (this would make the required reserves kept against the issued notes even less).The clearing house made sure every goldsmith in its system had enough gold in reserve to carry on this "fractional reserve" thing. Governments in virtually every country showed a strong interest in the workings of the mints and their clearing houses – wars were never cheap – and got heavily involved in the whole process of money creation and management from the very start.

Technologies changed. Dennis began to issue the fake notes electronically – the bank, after assessing the credit risk of potential borrowers, instead of issuing paper receipts to Vinny in a hush-hush environment, would open an electronic deposit for him and brag about it, maybe even publish a "tombstone" in the local newspaper if the borrower is rich and famous... These electronic deposits would then be transferred – obviously electronically – between banks in Venice and Genoa; the banks would agree to accept each other's fake notes (this was in their best interest, collectively, even if they competed with each other individually) and this would become the payment system. The name for the fake notes would change to "inside money" or "bank money" or "credit", the name of the gold on reserve with the clearing house – "base money", "high-powered money" or just "reserves". After 1971 gold had to be replaced with two-bit data structures, because America blew its gold on blondes and booze, made bad deals and got into the wrong brawls; the two-bit data structures would occasionally be printed on a special, hard-to-counterfeit paper; Dennis would change his name to "JPMorgan", the clearing house – to "Federal Reserve", but the fundamentals of commercial banking would remain the same – today, just as they were in 13th century Venice:

- Deposits at commercial banks are not *really* money, they are claims against the bank, convertible into money; they are IOUs of the bank to the customer – opposite to what everyday experience has led people to believe. When a customer puts cash into her bank account, she transforms "real money" (Federal Reserve notes) into a claim on her bank. As long as the claims are transferred electronically from one bank customer to another bank customer – these claims on the banks work as money, and no one is able to tell the difference between the claims on the banks and the real money (and in reality such difference does not exist – at least not until the bank goes under and everyone lines up in front of its office to convert their claims into "real money"). And this is the essence of the payment system.
- Lending in commercial banking does create new money (opposite to what the vast majority of people may think) – with offsetting debt for the borrower, and against interest. A commercial bank is thus fundamentally different from a credit union, because a commercial bank creates new money, while a credit union only transfers existing money from savers to lenders.
- Money for the interest due on the newly created debt-based money is not created anywhere in the system – an artificially created scarcity of money which makes society ever more competitive, requires ever more debt to be issued, ever newer and ever bigger growth opportunities.
- It is very important that commercial banks are up and running so that payments for groceries, clothing – or for oil tankers and F-16s – can be made not in cash but electronically.
- Commercial banks use short-term funding through deposits (as one funding venue), but make longer-term loans, creating balance sheets which may be, time-wise, out of balance.
- Banks are susceptible to panics. If depositors for any reason fear that their bank deposits are not safe, and start withdrawing deposits, this may indeed ruin a fractional reserve bank if no further measures are taken.
- The core business of commercial banking is evaluation of credit risk. Fundamentally, this is an IOU trade – an entrepreneur would offer the bank her IOU, if the bank accepts it is good, will provide its own, widely acceptable IOU, to the borrower (i.e. open up a deposit for the borrower), keeping the borrower's IOU as an asset plus a collateral in case of default on the customer's IOU.

"It should be clear that modern fractional reserve banking is a shell game, a Ponzi scheme, a fraud in which false warehouse receipts are issued and circulate as equivalent to the cash supposedly represented by the receipts."

Murray Rothbard

How the money creation process works: an illustration

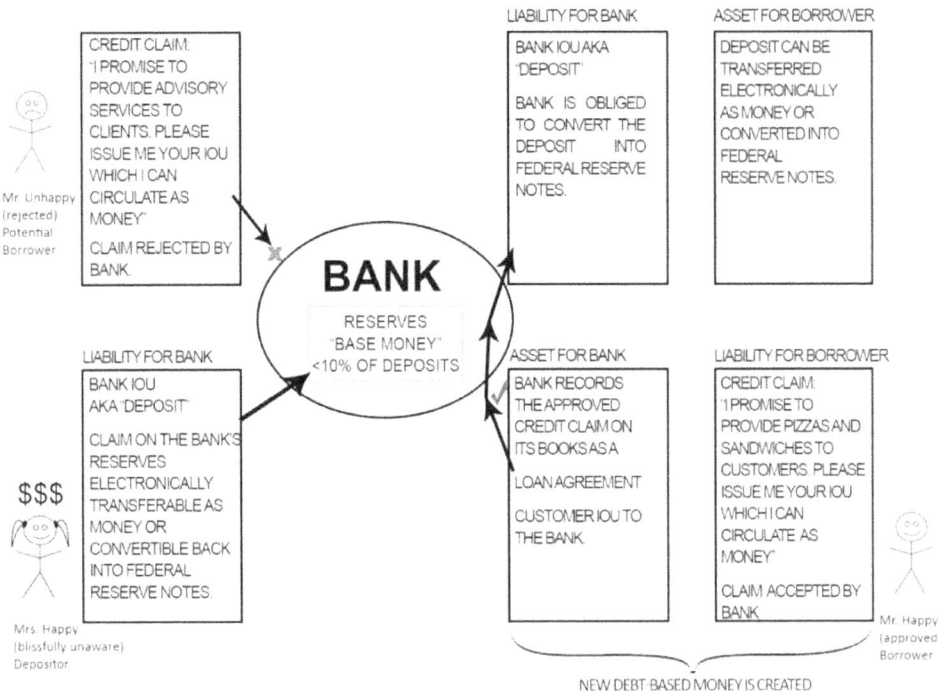

Let's look at the essence of the actions of each economic actor on the illustration:

1. *Mrs. Happy (blissfully unaware) Depositor.* She puts her money into the Bank. By this, she exchanges her Federal Reserve notes for a claim against the Bank (a customer deposit). The deposit essentially is a promise by the Bank to convert the deposit back into real money (Federal Reserve notes). Mrs. Happy is usually unaware that her money is (1) already gone, she owns not money but claims against the bank, and (2) the FDIC myth applies only in case a relatively small bank goes under, in case of a cascading bank failure the tiny percentages of all deposits that banks pay into the fund are insufficient to cover the losses of all "insured" depositors. No new money is created in this case, but the bank's ability to create new money is enhanced as it keeps less than 10% as reserves against all new deposits (loans) created.

2. *Mr. Unhappy (rejected) Potential Borrower.* He makes a credit claim to the Bank, that, for example, he will provide advisory services to investors, and wants the Bank to accept that IOU (the promise that advisory services will be delivered in the future), and wants the Bank to provide in exchange its IOU (the promise that the Bank will convert its IOU into base money). The Bank, however, decides the customer is not good for the claims he makes, and refuses to accept his IOU in exchange for its IOU. No new money is created in this case.

3. *Mr. Happy (approved) Borrower.* He makes a credit claim to the Bank, that, for example, he will provide pizzas and sandwiches to customers, and wants the Bank to accept his IOU (the promise that pizzas and sandwiches will be delivered to customers), and wants the Bank to provide in exchange its IOU (the promise that the Bank will convert its IOU into base money). The Bank decides that the customer is good, so the Banks accepts the customer IOU as its asset, issues its IOU to him (a deposit – Bank's liability and customer's asset). The customer can then circulate electronically that bank's IOU as money within the economy. New debt-based money is created in this case – and this accounts for some 97% of all new money creation in society.

4. *The Bank:* (1) evaluates credit claims made by potential borrowers; (2) those claims it approves are accepted as bank assets, in exchange for issuance of a bank IOU (a deposit in the name of the customer), which deposit can be circulated electronically as money within the economy, or can be converted into Federal Reserve notes (base money) by the customer; (3) the bank makes sure the borrower makes good on his credit claims and indeed backs up his IOU with its goods and services. (4) the bank can lump together many of the IOUs it has accepted and sell them to investors, freeing up liquidity for new loans, aka "securitization". (5) for new money to be created, someone must go into debt with the bank.

COMMUNITY CURRENCIES: CREATING MONEY WHEN THE BANKS ARE CLOSED[7]

It was during times of monetary distress, when the official funding channel – banking, often along with the legal tender currency – were unavailable due to war, hyperinflation, or due to bankers' risk-aversion, when entrepreneurs, in the private and public sector alike, realizing they couldn't promise repayment of debts in legal tender, promised what they *could* provide – *their* goods and services – and issued Deli Dollars, Farm Dollars, Rail Marks, coal money, etc. – as claims on their own future output. The notes they issued were either sold at a discount for the legal tender, or were used to pay directly contractors, employees. The entrepreneurs invented a peer-to-peer channel for debts settlement, and, unlike in the case of Dennis, it was not based on misrepresentation:

Frank Tortoriello, proprietor of a cafe in Great Barrington, Massachusetts, couldn't raise from banks the $5000 he needed to relocate his cafe, so he printed his own "*deli dollars*" with a value of $10 of sandwiches each. The notes were redeemable for $10 worth of deli food once the café was up and running. He then sold these notes for something like $8 each to prospective clients. He raised $5000 in a month. The interesting thing is that even the bankers who refused the loan on purely commercial basis, bought notes, personally supporting Frank's initiative!

Another example is the *German rail money*, issued in by the German Reich Railway in the 30's. In dire need of funding, and unable to obtain bank financing, the railway issued notes redeemable in its transportation services. The notes were used to pay contractors and suppliers, were made out to the bearer and in denominations convenient for circulation. They could be resold by their holders at any time to anyone for any price, but the Railway was obliged to redeem them at their nominal value, regardless of the market rate.

Again in the 30's, in the Austrian town of *Worgl*, hyperinflation had destroyed the local economy, leaving some 30% of the workforce unemployed, 200 families penniless. The mayor of the town, Michael Untergugenberger, facing a liquidity crisis in the town's budget, issued a new currency, the Worgl. The Worgl carried a demurrage charge (the currency slowly reduces its value over time), at 1% per month, affixed as a stamp on the Worgl note, in order to accelerate its circulation. The result was nothing short of an economic miracle – the town was back to full employment, a variety of public projects got completed, even taxes got paid ahead of time, believe it or not! American economists and senior foreign public official went to visit the economic miracle of Worgl. The system began to spread. At this point the Austiran Central Bank, concerned with the preservation of the status quo, had the project shut down. Almost overnight, the town went back to 30% unemployment.

Coal output was used to back the currency of the coal mine of The Wara Trading Company in the German town of Schwanenkirchen, a town devastated by hyperinflation. Again, the currency became widely successful, with over 2000 corporations accepting it, and again the Central Bank intervened to shut down the currency.

The list of currencies issued by businesses and backed by their goods and services is long. The fundamental logic, though, is the same. A business can issue an IOU in exchange for resources from the economy – as a promise to provide its own goods/services, if and when presented with the IOU, in the amount of the IOU[8].

A scholar from the so called Austrian School – Friedrich Hayek – proposed that free choice in currency would be the best long term guarantee of the stability of the money system. Friedrich von Hayek put the concept forward in articles, books and lectures around the 70's – namely, that denationalization of money and competition among currencies is the best guarantee for the long run stability of the monetary system. Economists, however, agreed that in a large community it is very hard to know which issuer is good and which issuer isn't, i.e. the "currency discovery costs" at the time were prohibitively high. This was back in the 70's though – when Elvis was still alive, and girls could throw their bikinis at him with admiration during concerts.

Then the Internet came along. And the Internet changes everything. Maybe it's time to reconsider the admirable work of von Hayek again. Hold the bikinis. Maybe it's time to "like" an IOU on Facebook:

---

[7]Most of the examples in the chapter are from the book "Stamp Scrip" by Irving Fisher, and "Rethinking Money" by Lietaer/Dunne

[8]The mutual credit clearing systems have been developed in the works of E.C. Riegel, T. Greco, P. Grignon, M. Linton, etc.

WIKIPEDIA – THE BEGINNING OF THE END FOR COMMERCIAL BANKING

Let us for a moment compare the centralized model of Encyclopedia Britannica (E.B.) and the decentralized model – Wikipedia, both dealing with evaluation of claims about the state of the world around us:

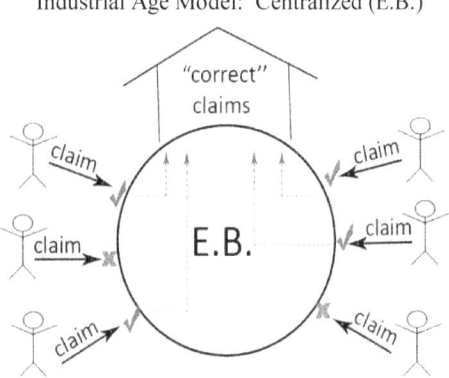

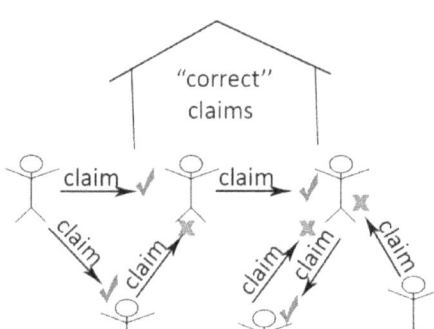

The decentralized model provides more, better, faster, cheaper results than its centralized counterpart – E.B.

Now, let's forget about Wikipedia and return to **commercial banking**. Let's take a bank in Europe somewhere, say a bank called "European Bank" (E.B.). As previously explained, a commercial bank deals with evaluation of credit claims of potential borrowers:

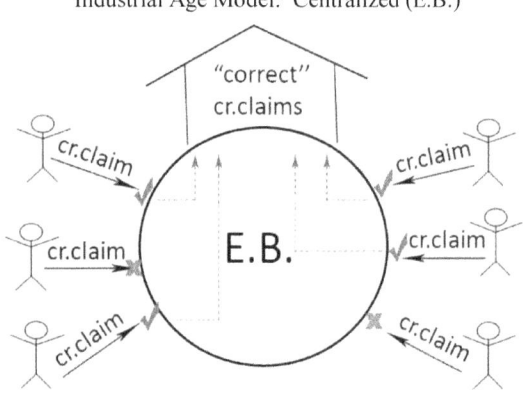

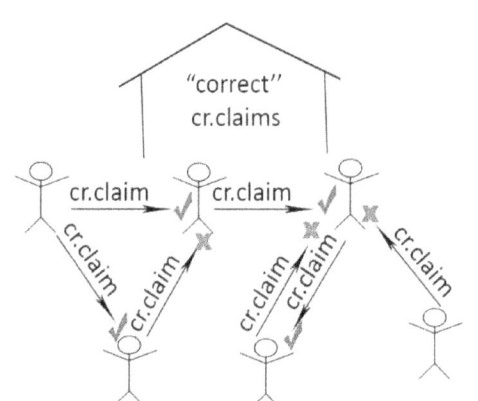

The decentralized model provides ....
.... results than its centralized counterpart – E.B.

Here is a test for the banking community:
  A) Identify if there are any similarities between the models above, and the models below;
  B) Fill in the blanks to the best of your ability.

It is the same underlying model: the use of the power of collective intelligence. Could the collective filtering system that cleanses Wikipedia from general claims without merit be used to cleanse the money system from credit claims without merit? The IT tools that would structure the processes in the bottom right corner are provided in section "Store of value defenses" later in this book.

THE EVOLUTION THAT NEVER HAPPENED: MONEY AND SOCIAL PURPOSES

How money works for social purposes – (1) begging

Imagine a community of 5000 very nice people. It has its Mr. Government at the top, Mr. Central Banker, Mr. Commercial Banker 1, Mr. Commercial Banker 2, Mr. Insurance Man, and a big fat Mr. ExxonMobil. And then there is little Alice, who is poor.

One day poor Alice got sick and needed to see a doctor.

It was to cost $50, and she didn't have any money. She started knocking on people's doors. The first home was the Jones family. "Hi, Mr. Jones. My name is Alice, I am 8 years old, and I am very sick. I need to be able to claim $50 worth of goods and services from our community – namely, a $50 medical check-up with the Good Doctor. I am asking 1 cent from you, just as I will ask from everybody else in our community". "Of course, little Alice" said Mr. Jones "We are nice, well-to-do people and we will not leave you without basic medical care. Here, take 1 cent".

Little Alice repeats the same thing 5000 times, goes to the doctor, pays him and everything ends up well.

The idea in Mr. Jones' mind that we are nice people, and that our society is wealthy enough not to let a poor girl without basic medical care is called "the social contract". Asking 1 cent from everybody is called "socializing the cost of the social contract". The particular process of funding the social contract described in this example is called "begging". Begging has no effect on the money stock of the community.

How money works for social purposes – (2) insurance

Mr. Insurance Man, seeing what Alice does, announced to the community "Listen up, people. If you all pay me in advance some money, I'll pay the good doctor should any of you get sick over the period of the year. I'll keep a little fee to cover my costs". Mr. Insurance Man is a clever one – he knows not everybody will get sick in a given year, so he is able to pull his little trick.

This is called "private insurance". Insurance has no effect on the money stock of the community.

How money works for social purposes – (3) taxation

Mr. Government, seeing Alice's travails, promises in his election campaign he will force everyone in the community to pay him some money, and then he – the good (!) Mr. Government – will pay the Good Doctor should somebody like Alice get sick. Mr. Government then hires a mean-looking Mr. IRS (everyone hates him and lies to him and avoids him at all costs), and a kind-looking Mr. Social Services guy.

The problem with Mr. Social Services guy is that he cannot efficiently reach every person in need of assistance, and the money Mr. IRS brings in is always tight. Both Mr. IRS and Mr. Social Services are expensive to maintain.

This is called "taxation". Taxation shouldn't have direct effect on the money stock – but indirectly might, as Mr. Government, if deep in debt, calls his buddy Mr. Central Banker asking him to twist the monetary system – just a little, and just once! – and print some money out of nothing, even if impoverishing everyone who holds money by diluting the existing claims on the community's real wealth (not to worry, no one ever finds out about this anyway).

How money works for social purposes – (4) commercial banking

Little Alice, instead of (1) begging, (2) taking out insurance, or (3) using a government social program, could go to Mr. Commercial Banker 1 and say:

"Hello Mr. Commercial Banker 1, my name is Alice, I am 8 years old and I am sick. I need to go to the doctor. It is to cost $50. Since I do not have any money, I thought I might give the Good Doctor an IOU for this amount, but he wouldn't have my IOU – he doesn't know me and cannot evaluate my credit risk. Could you please evaluate my credit risk, then I'll issue an IOU to you, and you will issue *your* IOU on my behalf to pay the Good Doctor. Everyone accepts your IOUs. The Good Doctor can then cash it if he wants to or keep it with his own banker"

"Sure, Alice, you've come to the right place" said Mr. Commercial Banker 1. "I've been authorized by Mr. Central Banker and Mr. Government to issue just such IOUs. I issue them against my reserves (the ones I keep with Mr. Central Banker), as electronic customer deposits, and everyone accepts them because everyone trusts me. So, I'll newly-issue IOUs for you, as *your* electronic claims on my reserves, in the amount of $50, and make a record stating you owe me $50. Through electronic transfer of your claims on me you will be able to buy goods and services from our community for that amount – because everyone in our community trusts me and knows I'm good for the money. Or, you could convert your claims on my reserves (your deposit of $50) into Federal Reserve notes – real money! – right away and pay the Good Doctor cash. Now, in fairness to the community, you'll need to eventually bring in an equivalent amount of claims back to me and we'll then destroy them – the $50 you bring back and the record of your debt to me; thus the original balance between you and the community in terms of claims on real wealth will be restored. Another reason to come back with an equivalent amount of claims is that when you instruct me to transfer the IOUs I've issued to you, I also transfer out an equivalent amount of my reserves – the real money I keep with Mr. Central Banker – and I'll need to bring my reserves back to normal. One last thing – I'll need a little something for me to cover my costs, called "interest". So once you spend the claims I'll create for you, you will have to go out there and work hard to obtain not only the amount of claims I initially created for you, but also take a few extra claims – that's to cover my interest. But please note – every dollar is created somewhere for interest, but no one creates the dollars for the interest itself! There are never enough dollars out there! That's how the system works – via artificial scarcity. It creates ever growing indebtedness and scarcity of money! Funny isn't it. So you'll have to compete, because someone is bound to be left without enough dollars – make sure it's not you! Use all the oil you can, fight for it if you have to, I don't care if you pollute the environment – but come back with the money. As a guarantee that you will compete, I'll keep your Barbie Doll, and if you do not come at the agreed time with the agreed amount – principal plus interest – I will sell the Barbie Doll and use the proceeds from the sale to destroy $50 worth of claims so as to restore the just balance in society, to return my reserves back to normal, and to keep my cut in this deal – my interest".

He then proceeded to set up an account for Alice, the account essentially saying Alice has a claim of $50 on him – he had plenty of reserves against which to issue IOUs. He then called Mr. Commercial Banker 2, where the Good Doctor keeps his claims against Commercial Banker 2 (i.e. has an account), and said:

"Hello Banker 2. Little Alice has a claim of $50 on me, and wants to transfer it to the Good Doctor, who has an account with you"

"Sure, no problem" said Commercial Banker 2."Transfer $50 of the real money (of the so called "reserves" – the ones we bankers keep with Mr. Central Banker) in my account with Mr. Central Banker, and I'll notify the Good Doctor that his claims on me increased by $50 because of a transfer originating from Alice through your bank, i.e. his deposit with me will increase by $50".

From afar, Mr. Central Banker looks on, making sure Commercial Bankers 1 and 2 keep sufficient "reserves" with him relative to the amount of deposits they keep on their books – so that they can safely issue IOUs and transfer claims (i.e. deposits) back and forth. Being the captain of the money stock of the community, he thinks "Hmmm, maybe I should raise the interest rate to discourage Alice from borrowing money again – too much credit is being created, prices are going up, this may get out of hand, and if prices change too much too fast, no one will bring their cows to the market!"

The commercial banking route is not a very humane route in the case of Alice – unlike the begging route which relies on our human nature, our compassion, on the values our grandmothers and preachers taught us. But it is nevertheless a viable, just, competitive, route. It is for customers who are willing, able and ready to compete, to do whatever it takes but to bring back to Mr. Commercial Banker 1 the promised principal plus interest. It is not for little girls, though.

How money does *not* work for social purposes – (5) central banking

Theoretically, another alternative for Alice exists – a very humane one, within the lines of the begging route. She goes straight to Mr. Central Banker and says:

"Hello Mr. Central Banker. I am only 8 years old, I am sick, have no money, and need $50 for a medical examination. Of all my options, (1) begging is unethical and doesn't scale, (2) I have no money for private insurance, (3) the government is broke, and (4) I cannot compete with Mr. ExxonMobil for the always insufficient (artificially scarce) dollars in circulation as required in a commercial bank loan. But I just went to everyone in the community, and everyone agreed to become one cent poorer if this will help me out – they called it "the Social Contract". Could you please issue me $50 *net of debt*? Oh, and I got Mr. Government to include this in your charter"

"Sure, little Alice. If that's the social contract, and Mr. Government allows me to do it, why not – let me print your $50, here – take it, pay the Good Doctor, and you are free to go and play with your Barbie Doll – it is mortgage free, and you are debt free. We all together, as a society, paid for your medical check-up". "It's a wonderful life" thought little Alice. "And maybe my $50 issued net of debt is exactly what is needed for all those people competing tooth and nail all the time for the interest that Mr. Commercial Banker wants from them but no one creates anywhere in the system."

The End

—————————

Options 1,2,3 and 4 are all viable options existing in real life. Option 5 – creating money net of debt for social purposes isn't – because of something done back in 1913, when a group of bankers got together, thinking how to issue the maximum amount of claims against themselves against a minimum reserve base, and at the same time come up with the money should everyone show up and ask for it simultaneously. So these men created Mr. Central Banker to help them out, but they created Mr. Central Banker in order to protect *themselves*, not little Alice. Not that it was some deep dark conspiracy theory, it rather wasn't – they did what was required to protect the monetary and banking system, as it existed back then, from the recurring nasty bank runs. Little Alice was – and still is, for better or worse – Mr. Government's problem, not Mr. Central Banker's problem.

> **Competition is built into the current monetary architecture, cooperation isn't.**

If a programmer were to look into the whole process, she would think "I can automate Option 5. If a poor little girl goes to the doctor, new money can be issued on the spot at the point of sale (the medical check-up), and there is no need for Mr. Insurance, Mr. Commercial Banker, Mr. Central Banker, and Mr. Government, Mr. IRS, Mr. Social Services. It will be a peer-to-peer transaction – between the little girl (the recipient of the service), the doctor (the service provider and the payee) and the society (the payer for the service) – all intermediated and executed via software. Bots will measure the CPI, and via the Demurrage Bot (negative charge on the currency) will reduce the amount of money in circulation so as to achieve the monetary goals as they are pre-set by society".

—————————

Why is it that we learned to equate "capitalism" with ruthless competition only – synonymous with consumerism, individualism, ego, elitism, dog-eat-dog, survival of the fittest? Why should individual freedom and property rights be incompatible with values like compassion, cooperation, mutual help? Why should "money" be almost a dirty word, almost leaving an uneasy feeling in your stomach? Why not have a money system that rewards cooperation while simultaneously freeing the competitive human spirit? Why not have a money system which combines competition *and* cooperation as its guiding philosophies? Darwin was right, 100% right that *within* a species it is "survival of the fittest", but it was Lamarck who demonstrated that it was the cooperative *species* that prevailed in the long run, species whose members learned to help each other while letting their winners charge ahead. Socialism was indeed, as Winston Churchill put it with characteristic eloquence, "an equal sharing of miseries", and a socialist economy with its competitive spirits dead is a permanently depressed economy. Capitalism run wild, however, brings its self-destruction too, albeit for a different reason.

FLAWS OF THE EXISTING MONEY SYSTEM: SUMMARY

1. **Money is created as debt** *only,* **against interest**. 97% of all money is put into circulation via creation of interest-bearing bank debt, causing, quite predictably, a perpetually indebted society. Since the interest on the debt is largely not created, it must be extracted by a debtor from other debtors, meaning (1) new debt must be issued in ever increasing amounts to prevent collapse of the whole system; (2) members of society are in constant competition for ever larger interest payments; (3) new sources of growth must be constantly identified and realized. It is for these reasons that resource depletion and resource-based conflicts become inevitable, as well as negative externalities such as global warming and pollution – people have bills to pay, you know. The ever-increasing neediness and competitiveness implied by this particular monetary architecture would be best summarized by a theologian as the proverbial "love of money" - and of course the root of all evil. As previously explained in the book, the problem is not with debt-based money issue *per se*, the problem is that this is essentially *the only* way of putting money into circulation.

2. **"Two-bit dictator" monoculture[9] of the money unit**. A "two-bit dictator" was a term used by US officials in the past to describe Hugo Chavez. The same term would perfectly fit virtually any legal tender currency in use throughout the world today – existing currency units lack depth of informational content and do not allow for any meaningful competition because of the existing legal tender laws. This "monoculture" aspect drives fragility and cyclicality into the economic system that is built on top of the money system.

3. **The money system is top-heavy, centrally managed**. A centralized network architecture is inherently unstable – it carries the risk of a failure that will affect the whole system; creative destruction is not allowed at the micro-scale, which means mistakes add up unnoticed. Capitalism's current money system has a monetary collapse built-in: the destruction of the money unit, destruction of money as a relationship management tool – evidenced in hyperinflation, complete loss in the currency, collapse of money-intermediated exchange.

4. **The optimum quantity of money is managed via barbaric instruments.** (1) central banks kill the economy across the board to reign in the money supply – akin to a medieval doctor bleeding a patient; (2) in bad times central banks cannot efficiently combat hoarding, i.e. cannot force the commercial banks to go out and lend.

5. **The money system is bank-centric, but fractional reserve banking is inherently unstable**. Banks are the institutional carriers of the money system, but banks are ever-susceptible to rational or irrational fears, "irrational exuberance[10]", shocks elsewhere in the economic/financial/political systems.

6. **The privately-owned banking system issues new money for wealth-claiming opportunities** (speculation, derivatives) causing misallocation of capital and deformations within the economy – the so called "bubbles".

Ideally, there will be a one-to-one correspondence between real wealth and its representation – money. This is sometimes referred to as "the real bills doctrine". For example, it would be OK to issue new debt-based money to build a new house – the amount of real wealth increases with the amount of new money put into circulation. No inflation occurs because of that, money keeps its value. If, however, we want to buy a house *already built*, with the idea to resell it later, our behavior does not create new wealth for society as a whole – no new houses are built. What our economic behavior implies is that we think we are smarter than the current owner of the house, so instead of letting her own the house and enjoy its rising value, we buy it from her, enjoy the ride on the upside, and resell the house eventually. There is nothing wrong with one investor being smarter/dumber than another one – virtually every investor is assured to experience what it is like in either of these positions at one time or another. The problems come from financing speculation with newly issued money – such a monetary behavior bears very high risk of inflating bubbles within the economy. If we all believe that house prices (tulips, bitcoins, etc) can only go up, then this belief, combined with the ability to issue new money for

---

[9]The risks and benefits of a monoculture in the monetary system are discussed in various works by Bernard Lietaer
[10]Alan Greenspan

wealth-claiming activities (speculation) means our expectations become self-fulfilling. House prices indeed do go up as long as we believe they do – and it is easy to make it happen if new money can be issued for such purposes – as long as the money issuers (the banks) are under pressure to get into the party and make the most of it for their investors – well they will – issue and issue and issue new money via new real estate loans – especially if they can quickly unload these loans via securitization on the financial market, hoping to have transferred the risk of default out there somewhere… And even if the banks are smart enough to see the bubble, they may hope to exit the party before the last call – you be the judge here… Financing speculation with newly issued (debt-based) money can build dangerous debt-fuelled bubbles, and when the bubbles pop, asset prices are destroyed, but the debts are not. As debts are not serviced, banks' assets are destroyed, they become insolvent, not to say panics and bank runs are possible, adding liquidity pressures to solvency problems; the payment system gets killed too. Issuing new debt-based money for wealth-claiming activities (as opposed to wealth-creation activities) is a recipe for the formations of very dangerous economic cancers/financial powder kegs.

7. **The money units bear no standard of value** – the dollar/pound/yen/etc. do not represent any standard of value – commodity, labor, basket of consumer goods, energy – nothing. An existing money unit is just a number. It doesn't mean anything, except that it is one more claim on the total real output of wealth of the country issuing it. This makes it (1) easier to manipulate and (2) harder to interpret it in everyday life (no one goes around knowing in their head what the total output of the US economy is, and what the total money supply is, hence what a "dollar" really means).

8. **The system has no anchor** for its "store of value" function. Gold used to perform that function with a high degree of efficiency and predictability. With the closing of the "gold window" by President Nixon in 1971 the link between the (so-called) paper money and gold was severed for good. The world has gone "fiat", and the store of value function of money depends on the decisions of central bankers and government officials.

9. **Government is heavily involved in the money system**, restricting democratic freedoms within society, causing depreciation of the monetary unit, enabling wars, currency wars, and trade wars.

10. **Unstable velocity of circulation**. Since profit is the fundamental driver behind new money creation by the banks, there is a pronounced tendency for high velocity (overheating) during boom times, and hoarding (freezing) in bad times. Some describe this as "manic-depressiveness" of the money/banking system – it makes the good times too good, and the bad too bad.

11. **Interest creates preferential attachment and short-term economic behavior** – (1) interest is the instrument for the trickle-up economics – transfer of wealth from the poor to the rich, and the rich are ever-likelier to be getting richer, whereas the poor are ever-likelier to stay poor(er). The resulting poverty and inequality destroy communities and individual lives, drive people to anti-social behavior, have people question the justice of capitalism.(2) The NPV calculation for an interest-bearing currency encourages short-term thinking on behalf of economic actors, negatively affecting sustainability for the planet as a whole.

12. **The payment system is exposed to credit risk, maturity transformation risk and other risks**. Some "systemically" important banks simply must exist if society is to be able to simply transfer large amounts of money fast around the economy.

13. **Maturity transformation against a fractional reserve creates instability**. Borrowing short and investing long, in the commercial banking system or in the "shadow" banking system is inherently risky, bank runs are always possible, and no one can predict how severe the contagion effect will be.

14. **Money is nationalistic** – money is mostly country-specific, leading to "monetary nationalism", currency and trade wars. One of the main reasons for creating the euro was political – the desire to stop centuries-old history of European wars and bloodshed.

Technological progress during the Primitive Age – the first tools made of wood, stone, bones – allowed higher productivity, specialization, hence division of labor that gave rise to the first exchange processes, aka the "economy" (from Greek – rules of the household). Barter might have been some initial solution only in very simple, limited economies; the costs of barter skyrocket as economies grow in complexity. Around that time the first IOU contracts must have come into existence – most likely as oral contracts - but the counterparty risks there must have been huge – these IOUs were difficult to enforce, illiquid, there was no way to find out how many of them the issuer had outstanding. Hence the necessity of some token of exchange, something that had value independent of the exchange process – and that's how money was born – as a tool to manage counterparty risk in the exchange process.

The self-interest of those entrusted with the safekeeping and management of the money unit brought about the invention of *credit* as a medium of exchange – the promise to eventually come up with that something having value independent of the exchange process. *Credit* enabled the great advances of the economy during the Industrial Age – the railroads, the factories, the skyscrapers, but *credit* also came with a fractional-reserve asset base, and as a debt system. Today, just as in the Pre-historic society, direct clearing of the exchange process is impossible – economic actors must bring their IOUs to a bank, where these IOUs are evaluated for soundness, then a bank IOU is issued, against interest, as medium of exchange for settlement of debts incurred during the exchange process. Thus, banks intermediate every exchange process out there in the economy, and interest is built into every transaction. But make no mistake – banks intermediate the exchange process for their own benefit, not for the benefit of the exchange process – just as any profit-maximizing enterprise is expected to.

This fractional-reserve, debt-based system of money and credit, however, has been empirically proven to be bubble-prone and unstable, and requires an obliging government and a Central Bank – to lend a helping hand in times of crisis. And lend they do – well into the trillions - as acting otherwise may mean a collapse in the very blood system of the economy. Also, due to the fact that interest is not created anywhere in the system, there are at any one time more obligations to eventually come up with exchange media (money/credit) than there is exchange media outstanding – an artificial scarcity of money that means ever more debt must be continuously issued, with ever larger payments accruing to the banking system. That goes well only as long as the economy grows faster than interest accrues on debt. An infinite growth on a finite planet is impossible, though – a debt-based system is bound to eventually self-destruct, collapsing the economy with it. A much more immediate threat, however, is the diminished ability of central banks and governments to prop-up ever-larger banking balance sheets – the socialization of the cost of the banking excesses has its limits, too.

Trillions upon trillions in bailout costs, crushing debt levels across the economy, an economy so laden with debt so as to be unable to withstand even minimal interest rate increases, an economy with little or no growth, government debt monetization, unfunded liabilities, depreciating fiat currencies, banking balance sheets exceeding the GDP, lavish (!) banking salaries – these are all symptoms of a debt-based system of money and banking that has grown too large within the economy, whose pursuit of self-interest is threatening the very economy it was supposed to lubricate. A similar phenomenon in living systems goes under the name of

---

CANCER

Luckily, the whole edifice of money and banking rests on one fundamental, crucial, hidden, overlooked assumption that has been taken for granted for centuries – namely, that exchange processes *must* be intermediated via something that has value independent of the exchange process in order to manage the counterparty risk in an exchange – and that is "money", and hence the existence of the banking system as the institutional, systemic manager of the system of money and credit. The purpose of this book is to show that Information Technology can empower economic actors to evaluate IOUs and manage counterparty risks on a peer-to-peer basis, eliminating the very *reason d'etre* for the existence of the banking system (at least in its current fractional-reserve debt-based form). And that includes not only gold and the whole gamut of conventional currencies, but also the Bitcoin, the Litecoin, and any other thing, notion, idea, concoction aiming at intermediation of the exchange process:

INFORMATION ABOUT THE EXCHANGE PROCESS IS THE BEST DISINFECTANT FOR THE PROCESS ITSELF

ENDGAME

"The next crisis will be bigger than the Fed"
Jim Rickards, author/investor

Governments across the globe are overleveraged. Staggering debt/GDP ratios are the new "normal". The debt levels are clearly unsustainable. The unfunded liabilities are a ticking time bomb, a harbinger of social unrest to come.

Central banks' balance sheets are overextended.

Banks are highly leveraged; have very large derivatives' books; sit on large positions of risky government debt; some nearly fail stress tests.

Inequality has reached histrionic levels.

Growth is sluggish or non-existent across the globe.

Competitive currency devaluations are becoming fact of life.

China and *Russia* face a host of internal economic problems.

The dollar is at risk of losing its international currency reserve status.

Interconnectedness across the globe transmits economic shocks across countries and continents.

War is rearing its ugly head in too many locations, globally.

Bubbles – in bonds, stock markets, currencies – have formed.

The *paper gold market* is likely manipulated, making correction down the road more likely and more severe.

Financial analysts, biblical scholars, commentators, writers, numerologists, your next door neighbor – there is too much (possibly self-fulfilling) talk about a coming collapse, about the system of paper money and banking.

These are the symptoms. The root cause - the disease - are the flaws in the ad hoc design of the money system currently in use globally.

The risks are too many, too great; at the same time the safety systems – governments' and central banks' balance sheets - are nearly destroyed. We are facing the risk that the next crisis may not be a crisis *within* the system, but a crisis *of* the monetary system itself – massive money printing will be the only possible solution, possibly resulting in hyperinflation, destruction of the store of value function of money, refusal of the economic actors to participate in exchange for the legal tender - a systemic crash.

"The money corrupting power of the state is manifested all about us...The nations of the world, in a conspiracy of ignorance, are pouring poison into their own economy and bringing about a universal breakdown of exchange through impaired media, forcing a return to barter, impoverishment and chaos"
E.C. Riegel "The new approach to freedom"

What's needed in such an environment is, parallel with attempts to stabilize the existing system, to direct efforts, via pilot projects, at the establishment of a new, better thought through, more humane, and most of all fractional-reserve independent money system – away from the current debt-based, centralized, nationalistic, fiat money system. The Internet provides the environment for it. The IT industry, via the Internet, can supply high quality, global, bank-independent and government-free money. The first cryptocurrencies – the Bitcoin, the Litecoin, etc.- have been the initial, albeit rudimentary from a monetary perspective, steps in this direction.

"How…can we establish a monetary system that is stable, free from irresponsible tinkering, and incapable of being used as a source of power to threaten economic and political freedom?"

Milton Friedman

"The monetary problem stands out today as the greatest intellectual challenge to the liberal faith. For generations we have been developing financial practices, financial institutions, and financial structures which are incompatible with the orderly functioning of a system based on economic freedom and political liberty"

Henry C. Simons "Economic Policy for a Free Society"

"The political money system is seen to be the channel of perversion for both the political and economic spheres"

E.C. Riegel "The new approach to freedom"

"Without stable money, the private profit system will some day go. This means that the bankers, as long as they insist on operating ….their (fractional reserve) 10% system, will be playing with fire. The best available safeguard against the overthrow of capitalism is the 100% system, combined with money management, to give us a stable dollar"

Irving Fisher

"The issuing power should be taken from the banks and restored to the people to whom it properly belongs"

Thomas Jefferson

"Of all the many ways of organizing banking, the worst is the one we have today… Change is, I believe, inevitable. The question is only whether we can think our way through to a better outcome before the next generation is damaged by a future and bigger crisis. This crisis has already left a legacy of debt to the next generation. We must not leave them the legacy of a fragile banking system too."

Mervyn King (Bank of England)

"There should be no monopoly of credit, no central authority with exclusive power to issue money, and no forced circulation of any currency….To truly empower a community, a currency must be issued on the basis of goods and services changing hands, i.e. it should be "spent into circulation" by local business entities and individuals who are able to redeem it later by providing goods and services that are in everyday demand by local consumers"

Thomas Greco "The end of money and the future of the civilization"

"The main thing we miss today is universal money, a standard of value, the link between the past and the future and the cement linking remote parts of the human race to one another"

Robert Mundell (Nobel Memorial Prize in Economics)

"How can power be dispersed, as it should be to preserve freedom, in control over money?"

Milton Friedman, C. A.E. Goodhart *"Money, Inflation and the Constitutional Position of the Central Bank"*

"There is a growing body of opinion that Democracy, in this country at any rate, has not been given a square deal. Its political power has been useless without real economic power. The view taken in this book is that its fatal mistake was first in allowing a private monetary system to grow up and then in not putting an end to it. It is finding itself under vague international compulsions to pursue policies which inflict irreparable damage to its internal economy, continuously to restrict production and employment, to get deeper and deeper into debt, and unable to use its strength or skill for its own life. After over a century's unparalleled advance in the arts of producing wealth, living is becoming for an ever-increasing proportion more difficult and insecure. Everyone knows that there is something wrong, and that the solution of the problem is not yet within the horizon of party politics.

The alarming increase of unemployment and the continued deep depression of our staple industries is the continuous theme of all parties, but on the money policy as the obvious, and indeed the definitely predicted cause, there is a conspiracy of silence. Parliament endorses and encourages the banker in his belief that the nation's money is his sole concern to create and destroy as he decides...

The public knows perfectly well that hardly any step in knowledge or advance in thought, however commonplace to-day, has ever been made without those deeming themselves authorities in the matter being hostile and opposed to it when first made. To regard money as made for man rather than man as made for money would, to the money expert to-day, be as great a heresy as it was at one time to believe and teach that the earth went round the sun and not the sun round the earth. But if Galileo and Copernicus had lived to-day, and had upset the theories of the authorities regarding the nature of money rather than of the universe, they would have had far more difficulty of getting their new views impartially discussed than they had from the Medieval Schoolmen and the Courts of the Inquisition.

Freedom of thought and discussion applies, as yet, only to the affairs of the mind and conscience which affect directly no man's pocket. It does not yet apply to money. That is the Ark of the Covenant, the Holy of Holies of the Slave Civilization. Those in authority know well the danger. It might have consequences to humanity graver and more fundamental than freedom of belief. It might lead to economic freedom, the tap root of all freedom, worth the name."

Frederick Soddy, "Money vs. Man"

MONEY AND CREDIT FOR THE INFORMATION AGE

"I hope it will not be too long before complete freedom to deal in any money one likes will be regarded as the essential mark of a free country"

Friedrich Hayek

QUANTUM MONEY MECHANICS

The field of Quantum Money Mechanics is about the money mechanics of the very small - of Papa Joey's Pizza, Carlo's Hairstyling, etc. It is the money mechanics of grandma Mary and grandpa Joe, of our local teacher, medical doctor, priest, yoga instructor, our friendly local neighborhood bank-of-issue *public* banker.

It is the money mechanics of a social contract coded via a Hayekian currency discovery process into a multidimensional information-based money system providing a medium of exchange, store of value, and a unit of account. It hedges a variety of downside risks for its users – hunger, poverty, unemployment, ill health, etc. - while assuring unlimited upside potential, i.e. equality in opportunity but not in outcome for its users.

It is a strange monetary realm. It has a bank of issue – the Quantum Bank - yet it is a bank that doesn't maintain a single customer bank account, a bank without reserves yet with never ending liquidity, a bank in which thought can give rise to money out of nothing; there is quantum entanglement between every quant; the more you slow down a quant, the more it dissolves into nothingness; and long term commercial debts are both dead and alive at the same time.

It is a peer-to-peer, decentralized, distributed money system, in which the power to create money – *Fiat Lux*[11] - and the benefit of seignorage (once the exclusive privilege of kings, emperors and princes) – is given into the hands of teachers, doctors, priests, coaches, artists, public servants, and entrepreneurs.

Name of Money System

Smart Electronic Currency System (SECS). The early adopters of the system can be reasonably expected to be geeks and young people, hence the need for a name which is fun, sexy.

Name of Currency Unit

Quant(a). A Quant bears a message that somewhere something good has happened – we all together, as a society, allowed an entrepreneur to bear the risk – and claim the reward – of a new invention, idea, vision. Or we helped a hungry person get a loaf of bread; or opened up opportunities for a poor child through education, or took care of our sick and elderly[12]. The existing fiat currencies, in contrast, bear the message that someone somewhere went into debt. Finally, there is the mysticism surrounding everything "quantum" - the childhood fascination with all things magical somehow never quite goes away.

Standard of value

1 Q = value of *an hour* of unqualified human labor of average intensity. Various standards of value are possible for a money unit: consumption standards (a basket of goods/services), a commodity standard (a single commodity or a basket of commodities), an energy standard (a unit of energy), a unit of some type of labor. The standard of value should measure a valuable resource, so as to encourage its wise use, and it should be easy to understand and interpret prices quoted in that unit. A unit of labor is a good choice because: (1) human labor is invested in every good and service we consume in our daily lives; (2) it is limited by virtue of our lifespans and amount of hours in a day; in a deeper sense, the quant measures *the* most important asset of them all – the time we are given on this Earth; (3) prices quoted in such a unit are very easy to interpret; (4) it gives a natural floor to wages, and with the Employer of Last Resort functionality[13], it eliminates much of the need of wage controls and regulation; (5) provides equalization of incomes worldwide at the low-income level (the value of a man's output sweeping the streets of Nairobi with a broom is the same as the value of a man sweeping the streets of Manhattan), and (6) drives home a very important point – that the only way to increase real wealth is to make sure that, (1) through technological advancement, those brooms get smarter and replace unqualified human labor, and that, (2) through education, the human behind the broom is elevated into a more productive capacity.

---

[11]"Fiat Lux", the text from the Book of Genesis, as used metaphorically by Lietaer/Dunne in "Rethinking Money"
[12]Here reference is made to the issuance of quanta by social algorithms, as explained later in the book
[13]More on the Employer of Last Resort is provided in part "Publicly issued net-of-debt credit" of the book

Demurrage

"Stamp Scrip[14] ... would be the best regulator of monetary speed, which is the most baffling element in the stabilization of the price level."   **Irving Fisher**, "Stamp Scrip"

The quant decreases over time – it rusts - a concept pioneered by Silvio Gesell a century ago. The general argument goes like this: if real wealth cannot be stored through time without incurring extra costs – real wealth may rot, rust, it needs storage, security, there may be all kinds of shrinkage – then money, representing real wealth, should have similar features. The fact that currently money does not decrease through time makes financiers absolutely unwilling to lend it unless they receive interest, and interest bears some rather serious consequences, as was previously demonstrated in this book. Whereas with real wealth, an owner of that wealth might be happy to just receive the equivalent real wealth in the future, being relieved of storage costs required for the transfer of that wealth forward in time.

Demurrage changes time preferences. The higher your liquid money at any present moment, the more you've got to lose now, the bigger your exposure to the Demurrage Bot – you are sure to lose cash if you try to stay in cash. In the quantum realm, what you need is not liquid resources, but productive resources – the demurrage has no effect on your factory, patent, diploma. Spend, invest, spend, invest – like there is no tomorrow – because, in the quantum realm, there will indeed be no tomorrow – at least for a tiny bit of your current money. And the longer term you invest – the less worry you will have when you yet again convert into cash at the end of your investment horizon. In contrast, current Net Present Value calculations discount heavily the future, making the case for sustainability rather … unsustainable.

In earlier experiments, demurrage on money has been demonstrated to significantly increase the velocity of money in circulation (people even paid their taxes in advance!). An attempt to hoard money – the root cause of deflation, one of the root causes of post-boom depressions – will make your money literally burn in your pockets in the quantum realm. The current advantage and general preference of liquid wealth over real wealth – of representation over reality - is gone in the quantum realm. You must make your money move around or you'll pay the price.

"Only money that goes out of date like a newspaper, rots like potatoes, rusts like iron, evaporates like ether, is capable of standing the test as an instrument for the exchange of potatoes, newspapers, iron and ether. For such money is not preferred to goods either by the purchaser or the seller. We then part with our goods for money only because we need the money as a means of exchange, not because we expect an advantage from possession of the money. So we must make money worse as a commodity if we wish to make it better as a medium of exchange."

Silvio Gesell, "The Natural Economic Order"

The existence of demurrage within the monetary system, however, does not exclude interest – far from it! Interest may still exist in the peer-to-peer transactions, when quanta already in existence are temporarily loaned among economic actors; interest may be built into transactions in the futures money market. In the quantum realm, interest exists but is not ubiquitous. Riskier money transfers will of course need interest as an incentive for their realization. It is liquidity preference per se, the proverbial love of money (the root of all evil), that is attacked by the Demurrage Bot.

Within an IT environment, the demurrage charge makes it very easy to control the amount of money via algorithms – by placing a negative feedback loop between the Consumer Price Index and the Demurrage Bot, so that the higher the inflation, the faster money is destroyed. The Demurrage Bot thus penalizes most the "idle rich" – those with accumulated large balances of quanta. In contrast, under the current monetary system, central banks must kill the economy across the board by raising the interest rate in order to reign in the supply of credit – akin to a medieval doctor bleeding a patient. The demurrage charge within an IT environment can allow tailor-made solutions for the optimum quantity and velocity of money within the economy.

---

[14]"Stamp Scrip" is the name given to demurrage-charged currencies due to the stamp that was to be periodically affixed to the notes – originally 2 cents on a weekly basis

Ways to issue new money in the quantum realm

(1)   new money is issued by providers of goods and services, as an obligation – in the form of a standardized IOU - of the issuer to redeem the IOU at par when and if the IOU is presented to the issuer for redemption. An IOU thus issued is freely transferable within the economy as money. This is in essence the currently existing working capital financing, only without the banking intermediation. The airlines' air miles, the supermarkets' loyalty points, etc., redeemable for the goods and services of the issuing business, are the early harbingers of the structured, standardized transferrable IOU used in the Quantum Money System for peer-to-peer credit clearing.

(2)   new money is issued by a public agency (the "Quantum Bank")*via debt* for the creation of new assets, the issue being *backed by the borrower's existing assets*. This is in essence the currently existing financing via long term loans under the commercial banking scenario with some adjustments;

(3)   new money is issued at the point of sale *net of debt* on the basis of need as per the social contract via the IT platform, by educators, doctors, priests, etc. This is a mechanism to encourage access to certain goods and services for members of society who would otherwise be unable to pay – like basic healthcare, basic education, pensions, etc. This is money not backed by any specific asset, except maybe the fundamental asset – a healthier, more educated, safer, calmer society that is prerequisite for the long run development of healthy businesses.

Money Taxonomy

Private (Commercial) Money (privately issued credit). Private money is issued by businesses, on their own initiative, as claims against their future productive output, as this output is evidenced by their quarterly revenues through the system. Commercial money is debt-based money, but it is very specific debt of the issuer – to redeem the quanta in the goods and services they provide. Commercial quanta carry default risk – the issuer may not be able to redeem them for a variety of reasons. Private (commercial) money can be rejected as a means of payment – i.e. it does not have "legal tender" status. Only the issuer of private money is obliged to accept his own money and redeem them at par.

Public Money (publicly issued credit). Public money is issued to businesses (as debt) for development of new assets, by the platform itself (the Quantum Bank), as long-term debt of the borrower, against collateral. In effect society, via the public Quantum Bank, provides the borrower with claims against itself, so that the borrower can create new wealth-generating assets. There is a repayment schedule, of course – at loan repayment dates commercial quanta of the borrower are generated within the Quantum Bank, as claims owned by society against the debtor, for the debtor's goods and services, via the Quantum Bank. It is important to note that this venue is for development of new assets only, and not for M&A, speculation – so as to reduce the pressure in the formation of debt-fueled speculative bubbles. There is also a big difference with the current commercial bank long term lending – in the commercial banking route at loan repayment dates credit is destroyed, while in the Quantum Bank's model public money is created once at loan origination, and then commercial money is created at loan repayment dates. Since this will most likely be inflationary, the Demurrage Bot destroys liquid wealth already accumulated, thus giving advantage to wealth creators and the public at large over the "idle rich".

Public money is also issued for social purposes (net of debt) by the so called "social algorithms" – as per the coded social contract – in cases when all of society has decided to pay for a specific good/service. For example, when money is generated for a retired person at the point of sale; or for health care of a poor person, or for education of poor students, or for public works under the Employer of Last Resort program[15]. Public money is not a claim on any specific business's output, i.e. it is not "backed" by anything except the enhanced human capital and the goodwill of a safer, healthier, better educated and more humane society. Public money does not carry default risk and is universally accepted, i.e. has "legal tender" status.

Private and public quanta have the same underlying IT architecture.

---

[15]The Employer of Last Resort algorithm is explained later in the book

Privately issued credit (peer-to-peer credit clearing)[16]

Currently, an entrepreneur in need of working capital financing cannot issue her IOUs directly to vendors, employees, etc. – an entrepreneur must go through the banking system, where her IOUs are (1) evaluated for soundness, then (2) the entrepreneur provides a guarantee to the bank in the form of a mortgage maybe, (3) the entrepreneur's IOU is provided to the bank as a loan contract, which becomes an asset of the bank, and then (4) the bank issues its IOUs to the entrepreneur – as a bank deposit convertible into Federal Reserve notes. These bank IOUs can then be presented by the entrepreneur to vendors, suppliers, etc. for payment of goods and services – either as a wire transfer to the vendor's bank (inside money, i.e. without conversion into Federal Reserve notes), or as cash – after a conversion of the deposit into Federal Reserve notes.

In the quantum economy, however, the evaluation of the entrepreneur's IOU is done on a peer-to-peer basis, and the banking intermediation is eliminated. Entrepreneurs issue their own IOUs, each IOU being a multidimensional data structure with several fields. These are the so called "commercial quanta" – claims against the entrepreneur's future output, and they constitute much of the money stock in the quantum economy. The issuing of commercial quanta by businesses is based on successful precedents with "Deli dollars", "Farm dollars" and other community currencies in the US, the "Rail money" of the German Reich Railway in the 30's, the wildly successful Wörgl in Switzerland, etc. It is essentially peer-to-peer working capital financing, without the intermediation of the banking industry. Here it is not for your banker to decide if your business is any good to deliver the goods/services – it is the person accepting (or rejecting) your money making that call. It is the power of your business (or your personal) brand – and it may be worldwide (Coca Cola), or it may industry-wide (Kleiner Perkins Caulfield Byers in the US venture capital community), or it may be in your neighborhood only (Papa Joey from Papa Joey's Pizza). The premise here is simple: a currency can only be backed by the productive output of its issuer – hot pizzas if issuer is Papa Joey's Pizza, haircuts if issuer is Carlo's Hairstyling. It *looks* as if the mighty US dollar is backed "by the full credit of the US government" – it is not. The dollar is only a content aggregator, of sorts - it's those pizzas and haircuts that back the dollar, collectively. An issuer can issue claims only on its own output of goods and services, whatever they may be – and if her word is her bond, she must redeem the claims she has issued – if and when they are presented to her for redemption by the bearer of the claims - at par.

A crucial bane in the history of banking in the 19[th]century, and for the Hayekian currency discovery process in general, has been the cost of the discovery process – actors in the economy had to invest time and effort to find out if the currency of the issuer was any good. With a variety of issuers, this becomes too great of a burden, and makes the whole process impractical. That's why free banking[17] during the 19th century was such a hassle – for a large country such as the US, and given the then-existing lack of reliable communication channels, there was no way to find out if a bank note from an unknown bank was any good – for customers and other banks alike. There were fly-by-night operators, the so called "wildcat banks" who would come on the scene, issue a lot of notes and then disappear without a trace, or there were fake notes, or simply notes from banks too far away to know them well. There were businesses maintaining lists of banks with samples of their notes, providing guidance as to which issuers are reputable and which are not. But these quality control systems were too slow, too inefficient, too cumbersome; hence the need for standardization of reserve requirements, and note standards, and hence the Central Bank as regulator and protector of the standards. For a while free market proponents claimed competition will help regulate the market for notes issuance, and competition indeed can do miracles to separate the chaff from the wheat, and that includes monetary economics as evidenced in Hayek's work; but without reliable information for decision-making and proper feedback mechanisms "competition" disintegrates into "free for all", chance and chaos, and the damage caused by the "free for all" can outweigh the advantages of the competitive, free entrepreneurial environment. With advanced IT, however, the currency discovery costs can be brought down to the cost of computer processing time, and the spirit of freedom and competition can be safely released to do its magic. The next chapter demonstrates how the Hayekian currency discovery process can be implemented in practice within an IT environment as a first line of defense for the "store of value" function of money.

---

[16]Based on the work of E.C. Riegel
[17]Organization of the banking industry without a Central Bank

"Store of value" defenses for the Quant

The "store of value" function of money had been ensured during most of the Industrial Age - until the early 70's - by linking a fixed amount of currency units (dollars for example) to a fixed amount of a durable, relatively scarce mineral described in Mendeleev's Periodic Table of Elements with atomic number 79 and symbol "Au" – commonly referred to as "gold".

The existence of gold in the Universe is no doubt an act of God.

The existence of gold in the monetary system of man is no doubt an act of Man.

Not only it is an act of Man – it is an act of Man from an age when the Earth was still presumed to beat the center of our Universe.

Curiously enough, the misconception that the Earth is flat and a God-given center of the Universe has been easier to overcome than the misconception that gold is "precious" in itself and a God-given center of our monetary universe.

There is nothing precious in gold per se, except in our teeth and on our fingers/ears/chests. What has been indeed precious in gold throughout the centuries are the *functions* that gold carried out for so long in our money system. Horses were not that valuable per se – their *transportation function* was. Oxen were not that valuable per se – their *plowing function* was.

There is a multi-billion-dollar market that IT can take down – the gold market. The stockpiles, the mining companies' securities, the bullion banks, the open contracts, the derivatives – are all vulnerable to something that can carry out the monetary function of gold in an infinitely better way than any clumsy physical substance:

ALGORITHMS

Algorithms with names such as "Inflation-buster" and "Printer-sprinter".... and if these names sound like something that has been invented by people who still play computer games in their Moms' basements – that's because they *were* invented by people who still play computer games in their Moms' basements. People too young to know there once was a "gold standard" – and who couldn't have cared less about it. Keeping the value of a digital currency of an issuer constant is nothing that would make any electronic game developer break a sweat.

Preserving the value of money within the quantum money system takes place (1) at the individual level and (2) at the aggregate level. At the individual level, each issuer's outstanding currency is measured vis-à-vis the issuer's revenues and on that basis, along with some other metrics, users are allowed informed choice in currency. At the aggregate level, a negative feedback loop between the Consumer Price Index as measured by the system and the Demurrage Bot assures the optimum quantity of money in real time.

Let's see how preserving the value of money at the individual level has been designed to work in the case of our example – Papa Joey's Pizza:

Let's assume Papa Joey's Pizza can issue its own money, i.e. Papa Joey's Pizza commercial quanta, which quanta can be used within the economy as money (only with vendors willing to accept them, though!). An obvious temptation for Papa Joey would be to over-issue his Papa Joey's Pizza quanta – to issue more promises for future pizzas and sandwiches than he can possibly deliver. He gets the reward now by spending the quanta into the economy (the so called "seignorage", previously exclusive privilege of monarchs and central banks), yet he has to put in the redemption effort later, so – why not print some more quanta now and worry about it later. In this case, his notes will become somewhat less reliable – there are more promises made (notes outstanding) than there will be pizzas and sandwiches. If he over-issues, there is a strong doubt as to whether he will be able to redeem all the notes at face value – there will simply not be enough sandwiches to go around, and either some noteholders will go empty-handed, or every noteholder will get half a pizza or something. So, how can we guarantee that Papa Joey doesn't over-issue? Simple. Let's agree what is a reasonable measure of his ability to deliver the goods – how about his last month's revenues? Or maybe quarterly revenues? Semi-annual? Let's say he's good for three months' worth of pizzas and sandwiches - which means that if he issues 3 months' worth of revenues as deli money (i.e. Papa Joey's Pizza quanta), he's good, 100% good. Anything issued over and above that – and his whole note issue goes down in its coverage (aka "*backing*").

And that's precisely where IT comes in. The system continuously monitors Papa Joey's revenues vs. his outstanding currency, and publishes a simple, easy to understand metric - *% backing* (one of the fields of the commercial quant). At 100% (or more) Papa Joey's quanta are as good as gold – he can be safely assumed to be able to deliver his pizzas when presented with his currency. At less than 100% backing - well, it is not so sure if all those who hold Papa Joey's currency will get a full pizza…

Thus, each commercial quant within the Quantum Money System is a claim on the productive output of a specific issuer, and each commercial quant bears the mark of respectability – the % coverage, or *backing*. A quant at 100% backing says that the issuer has exactly 3 months' worth of revenues of outstanding notes; a quant at 60% backing means the issuer either has been too adept at his privately owned, commercial money printing press, or his revenues went down since he issued the quanta. A quant at 150% means the issuer has a very tight monetary policy, and can issue more of his money (and claim goods and services from the economy) – and will still be able to redeem everything at par.

Normally, a quant with less than 100% backing should trade on the money market at less than face value. But if you are about to use that issuer's goods/services, chances are you will first look on the money market for this issuer's money that trade below par, buy that money at a discount so as to redeem them at par with the issuer.

Another IT-generated metric for a currency's reliability is its "Cashrank" – each time a currency is used is logically akin to each time a link is made to a machine (PageRank), and with some other inputs Cashrank becomes a guide for the acceptance and reputability of a currency. Coca Cola, for example, assuming prudent monetary policy, would have a very high Cashrank, similarly Google, Apple, GE, etc. And while certain multinationals will enjoy wide acceptance of their money, small community business issuers will no doubt enjoy the pride and community-building spirit when their money is trusted by their regular patrons, neighbors, family members and friends – when community members act as economic actors empowered with freedom of choice, and with the correct and timely information for making the right choice.

Free choice in currency has been demonstrated to reverse Gresham's Law (the so called "Gresham's Law" is the notion that bad money drives out good from circulation, as people hoard the good money and spend the bad – in the past coinage would often get debased in various ways so as to diminish the content of metal used as money). Free to choose the best currency for them, and well-armed with adequate information for correct decision-making, rational economic actors naturally refuse bad money (and bad money remains hoarded with their issuers, and hence completely useless as media of exchange) and accept the good money. The practical operation of this process is well documented in the book "Good Money" by George Selgin about the experience of Great Britain in the 18th century with private coinage. Back then, however, the medium of exchange *had* to have a *material* carrier, economic actors *had* to *physically come together* for a decision-making meeting, in which to *vote by hand* in favor of the best issuer's coins (the Anglesey Company in that particular example). Fast forward two centuries, and we have at our disposal easy-to-generate data structures (as opposed to having to mine/process/melt/mold ores), iPhones, Facebook, Wikipedia - tools that could have made the Anglesey Company's job so much easier in terms of what to use as medium of exchange, how to circulate it, how to have it evaluated, rated, ranked, accepted, redeemed… IT, and the Quantum Money System in particular, does not change the essence of sound money – it only makes everything about it **so much easier**.

Thus, a commercial quant (Papa Joey's Pizza quant, for example) is a valid means of payment everywhere within the quantum economy - but the issuer is the only one *obliged* to accept it for redemption - at any time, at face value. Papa Joey's quanta can circulate round and round within the economy – if people trust them to hold their value (as evidenced by the backing percentage and related metrics).These quanta will go out of circulation when redeemed at Papa Joey's Pizza for pizzas and sandwiches - or until the demurrage bots destroy them completely over the years.

The big catch of the proposed IT-based monetary architecture is that irresponsible behavior of the person behind the private printing press will hurt – immediately, directly, the first and the most - the very people who trusted him with *his* money. Peer pressure has been demonstrated, again and again, to be one of the greatest motivators for human action, much greater than the orders of a boss or any authority figure: everyone who has accepted a businessperson's currency – these will most likely be the closest business partners, the employees, friends, family, neighbors – are designed within the quantum money system to become the guardian angels of the integrity of the monetary system. Using interconnectedness and IT, the quantum money system screams bloody murder each time a businessperson abuses her privilege with her privately owned printing press, by reducing the % backing of her currency. In the current monetary system, this would be the equivalent to have the dollar bills in our pockets shrinking with each successive round of QE by the Fed…wouldn't that be a sight! And not only the quantum money system shrinks the value of that businessperson's money, but chances are this rather unpleasant process will take place while the businessperson's money is in possession of those closest to her – business partners, employees, friends, family, neighbors – people best positioned to either help her raise revenues to re-establish full backing on the system, or inflict on her a "death by a thousand cuts" – provide negative feedback in a multitude of ways because that businessperson's overprinting made *them* poorer. Mario Draghi, "the eighth most powerful man in the world"[18], will never - never - come anywhere close to such awesome power – the power of the collective.

What we've just described is the concept of *emergence* – spontaneous order (sound money), arising out of individual actions based on local information only; the dynamic of the Invisible Hand working to weave individual rationality into a collectively superior outcome.

There is another topologically important point here - namely, that any centrally-planned network architecture – whoever the people on top may be - has the collapse of the whole system built into the architecture. So that when the alarm bell finally sounds for centralized systems – it sounds for the system as a whole, and boy is it ugly!

One of the reasons socialism failed, was that no one ever went bankrupt. In practice, there was no such thing as bankruptcy. And inefficiencies and malformations added up, and up, and up – until there was no bread in the stores and no electricity in homes. No one sounded an alarm when capital was misallocated, wasted, abused. "The government" was always there to patch things up. Workers stealing like crazy, working little if at all – no problem, there were more subsidies from the government. A factory built in the wrong place, selling the wrong products, at the wrong price – no problem, no problem at all….until eventually so many faulty economic designs added up that nothing could save socialism from itself. Too bad capitalism's current monetary design is way too socialistic, way too top-heavy, way too centralized. It went down on the watch of financiers like Alan Greenspan, John Mack, Ben Bernanke and Jamie Dimon – it will go down on *anybody's* watch.

The quantum money system, in contrast, is designed to recognize losers, abusers and freeloaders early, while they are still small and not systemically threatening – and then proceeds to kill them quickly, protecting the overall health of the commons. The quantum money system does give monetary freedom, yes – lots of it - but it is freedom coupled with tough justice via a very strong negative feedback mechanism ingrained at the very micro level of the network's architecture.

And then, at the macro level, the Consumer Price Index is calculated in real time, and a negative feedback loop with the Demurrage Bot protects the price stability of the economy and the purchase value of the quant at the macro level.

As to central banks' interest rate manipulations and gold - as tools for managing the optimum quantity of money, the velocity of money, the value of money – the time may be coming for such tools to take their rightful place in the museums of monetary history, along with the distinguished-looking pictures of central money planners such as our esteemed ~~Politburo~~ Central Bank presidents and FOMC members.

---

[18]Forbes

Quantum currency wars (example – pizza currency war)

It was a typical Friday afternoon…Walking around in his restaurant's kitchen, Papa Joey opened up one of the many cheese boxes stacked in the fridge and frowned. The cheese was not going to last much longer. On Tuesday he got a great offer from the cheese company, but acted maybe a little too impulsively – he overbought, it turned out, business during the week was slow, it was already Friday, and he knew he had only a day to sell the cheese…Taking out a pen and a napkin, Papa Joey ran a few numbers. He then punched a few buttons into his mobile device – and his Papa Joey Pizza quanta, formerly fully backed, were now quoted on the system at 87%.

"Ready for action, boys" he yelled at his staff. "We are going to get busy tonight"

At the same time, Don Joerr – a venture capitalist from the Valley - was scanning the San Francisco area on his mobile device planning the usual Friday evening out for his beer drinking buddies. Suddenly, his eyes lit up "There!" he thought, looking at the discount on Papa Joey's quanta. He spread the word immediately, and soon enough two minivans with guys looking for a great pizza and some great time on Friday evening pulled over in front of Papa Joey's Pizza.

"You see, Papa Joey is not a very sophisticated fella, money-wise" was explaining Don to his beer drinking buddies at the table. "I almost feel bad taking advantage of the old man. I mean, such great pizzas at such a low price..." The table cheered "Cheers cheers", obviously drowning any feelings of remorse with large quantities of beer. Strangely, Papa Joey was telling a different story to his chef: "These VC guys! They think they are so smart, you know. They probably think I'm stupid or something. But they forget we Italians invented banking! We even put our boy Mario on top of the ECB! Ha! I've priced the cheese at cost, but I make so much on the beer! These VC guys – so funny you know" Papa Joey was all smiles, too.

Everyone had great time. Papa Joey was happy, having sold all the cheese at cost but having made so much on the beer, Don & Company enjoyed great pizzas at a good discount, and everyone was happy and smiling.

One man, however, wasn't smiling – the owner of the Domino's Pizza franchise across the street. He saw the cheese company truck last week pulling at Papa Joey's, and all the cheese boxes Papa Joey unloaded into his restaurant. He thought then that the old man had lost it – yes, the cheese company was offering a great discount at the time, but there was no way you could sell that much pizza! Now, looking at his half-empty restaurant, and at all the fun going on at Papa Joey's, he knew all too well what was happening….Clenching his teeth, he made a few quick strokes on his personal device, and there – his quanta were down to 82%. "You won't be laughing tomorrow, old man" thought the Domino's Pizza owner.

Sure enough, next evening, Domino's was full, while Papa Joey was licking his wounds in a half-empty restaurant. Not one to be easily bulldozed, he replied in kind – another round of devaluation. Down to 75%!

Soon, the two restaurants were in a genuine currency war. They were working like crazy, yes – and losing their shirts. Customers were flocking in, redeeming cheap quanta for their full value at the restaurants, but the restaurants themselves had to buy supplies for full value. The two businessmen were bleeding each other into extinction…..After a while, the situation had become unbearable. The two businessmen met at the Local Trade Organization, trying to sort things out – no luck. As negotiations failed, in their anger, they placed boxes of tomatoes in front of their restaurants and started throwing tomatoes at each other. Soon, the whole street was overflowing with red tomato juice….

The End

Now – change Papa Joey Pizza for the US, the Domino's Pizza Franchise for China; the Papa Joey Pizza quant for the US dollar, the Domino's Pizza quant for the yuan; change the Local Trade Organization for the World Trade Organization; change tomatoes for nukes; and before you change the red tomato juice overflowing the city streets with you know what – you have all the reasons you need for transferring currency conflicts into the quantum realm, into the hands of people who have tomatoes but not nukes…

Publicly issued debt-based credit (credit for creation of new productive assets)

The Quantum Bank is the sole bank of issue for the Quantum Money System. It issues debt-based money. It's a public bank, but "bank" is a misnomer. It's more of a public agency, with a primary goal of assessing viability and credit risk of projects and ventures creating new wealth – new assets, goods and services for the economy. It extends long term credit to credit-worthy businesses against good collateral, and collects the proceeds of the loan on behalf of society, acting as a trustee on the loan. The credit is issued in newly created public space quanta. The borrowers deposit the money from the new loan with their own accounts within the space; nothing is deposited with the Quantum Bank – it does not contain a single customer account. It has only one account - its own, where claims against the borrowers are generated at each loan repayment date as loans become due. The funds thus accumulated in the Quantum bank are accessible to public officials for funding of public projects. The Quantum bank does not provide customer accounts of any kind, does not accept deposits and does not provide any wealth management services, nor any payment services. It does not maintain "reserves". It cannot experience a liquidity crisis – it has no liabilities whatsoever. It is always ready, willing and able to issue new loans to finance business. Its operation is completely independent of the financial system.

Wealth-claiming and redistribution activities (speculation, derivatives, M&A, etc.) can be financed on the peer-to-peer market with quanta already in existence. This policy aims to make the economy less prone to formation of easy-money, debt-funded bubbles.

Having approved a loan, the Quantum Bank provides borrowers with newly issued claims against society (public quanta). There is a debt repayment schedule, of course, just as it is currently with commercial bank loans – but there is a big difference at the repayment stage between the currently existing commercial banking model and the Quantum Bank's model: currently, as long term debts come due, they are repaid by businesses in legal tender to the commercial banks, and the commercial banks destroy that money (credit). In the case of the proposed architecture, as payments on the Quantum bank's long term debts come due, they simply become active commercial quanta on the Quantum Bank's books – claims owned by society (via the Quantum bank) against the debtor, *for the debtor's goods and services*. Thus, at each loan payment date, new commercial quanta spring into existence on the Quantum Bank's books as claims of society against the debtor's output. The newly activated commercial quanta may have % backing below, at, or higher than 100%, depending on the revenues of the debtor. The Quantum bank could then at loan repayment dates make one of three things:

a) redeem the maturing quanta for goods and services with the issuer, regardless of their % backing
b) keep the maturing commercial quanta on its books, where they will be available for public works, most likely in the debtor's area – if the quanta have approximately 100% backing and are hence acceptable as means of payment in society.
c) repossess the collateral of the debtor, sell it on behalf of society to make good on the promise of the debtor to restore the monetary balance *vis-a-vis* society (previously disrupted when the borrower was granted newly issued quanta - claims against society) – if the quanta are below 100% backing.

Most likely, the Quantum bank will, immediately upon extension of a new loan, turn around and resell the loan (all the quanta lying *in potentia* on its books*)* in the futures money market to private investors. This will have the effect of keeping the public Quantum bank *very liquid* at all times, as long as it manages to extend new loans. The securitization of the Quantum bank's loans will be taking place via the push of a button. The actual realization of the maturing commercial quanta will be a decision of the market – (a) redemption for goods and services of the issuer, or (b) release into circulation via purchasing of other goods and services (assuming 100% backing), (c) repossession of collateral (if inadequate backing), with the Quantum Bank acting as a trustee for creditors.

The key difference here is that successful long-term loans do not need to be repaid in "legal tender" - what is important is that the debtor use the loan proceeds to develop sufficient capacity to generate goods and services, and to grow sufficient revenues so as to be able to maintain 100% backing status for all his quanta – those issued by him/her as working capital, as well as those springing into existence, maturing from the long-term loan repayment schedule. The debtor's money stock in circulation will then increase with the maturing quanta, increasing the money stock within the economy. If this is inflationary, the Demurrage Bots will penalize the "idle rich" the most, in effect giving advantage to entrepreneurs and the public sector.

Several things become obvious from the explanation: (1) booming businesses will be flooding the economy with new, good-as-gold 100% backed quanta; while receding businesses and industries will be slowly reducing their money in circulation; (2) contrary to the status quo, where the destruction of money by the commercial banks at loan repayment protects those already rich (no dilution for their existing money), in the quantum economy the liquid savings of the "already rich" are constantly eroded by the Demurrage Bots with each and every successful new entrepreneurial project – so the rich must constantly compete and produce and innovate, or at least lend and invest – or else will eventually lose their wealth for sure - the quantum economy is unkind to lazy folks, no matter how liquid; this kind of arrangement benefits entrepreneurs and the public sectors over the "idle rich"; (3) businesses will be greatly facilitated by the fact that should their business grow to a sufficient size to keep their quanta fully backed by productive output, their long term loans essentially…. do not have to be repaid. Read that again if you have to. Yes. All entrepreneurs have to do is grow their business, and then grow again, and again.

Entrepreneurs will kill for a deal like that

….as will the public sector.

"Those engaged in initiating the new scale of production must be paid for by others abstaining to the same extent from consumption over the period required for the new scale of production to mature. Then, and continuously afterwards, every one may consume on the average at the new and increased rate of production. But for this to be possible, the money in circulation must then be correspondingly increased….

…Consumers have to be provided with money as much as producers for the system to work properly, the one providing the other in an endless circulation. Inability to distribute goods is as much a cause of poverty as inability to make them. Or, to put it the other way, poverty is due to inability to produce sufficient goods for national requirements, and this inability may be real technical inability or it may be purely artificial, due to the inability to distribute what has already been made. For many a long day now the poverty of this country has been overwhelmingly artificial…

…For as is only now becoming understood by people not professional financiers, the nation's money, is a mere by-product, as it were, of money lenders lending what they have not got to lend…To satisfy those who pretend they have lent it, it must be periodically drained out of the productive system, and the community instead of a live industry is left with a dead corpse."

Frederick Soddy "Money vs. Man"

Publicly issued net-of-debt credit (credit issued by social algorithms)

"The tramp is not a self-invented, self-developed, self-made brute; he is an evolution, and society is responsible for his brutalization, and the monetary laws of civilization have had the greater part in that evolution"

"The government supervisors capable of measuring the needs for currency of the various parts of the United States and the extent of the volume best suited to such needs, as well as the methods of getting the currency to them, are angels that have not yet been sent to Earth" **James A.B Dilworth** "Free banking, a natural right"

Social algorithms issue public quanta *net of debt*. Currently, only notes issued by a Central Bank are issued net of debt. The issuer of net-of-debt money enjoys the benefit of seignorage – the full purchasing power of the money created out of nothing and without a corresponding obligation.

Issuing money net-of-debt was demonstrated in example (5) How money does not work for social purposes – central banking, earlier in the book. To repeat briefly: if society agrees that certain types of transactions, for certain types of economic actors, must be paid for by society, one way to make everyone pay for such transactions is to issue new money specifically for these transactions, thereby diluting the existing claims (the money) of all money holders out there in the economy.

Currently, social programs are financed via government taxation and government borrowing. The disadvantages of this venue are obvious – large government bureaucracies, unsustainable government debt, inefficient coverage by the programs.

The Quantum Money System, however, could easily issue new quanta for social programs, achieving the goals of these programs while disintermediating the government from active management of these programs, transferring entitlement programs from fiscal to monetary policy. Basic rights we feel everyone should be entitled to – basic education, basic healthcare, basic legal protection in a court of law, the bare necessities of life, creating and raising children, old age security – can be provided for the poorest members of society, by the society at large, via money printing by the social algorithms:

Elimination of hunger
Assume we want to make sure that no one in our society goes hungry – regardless of whether or not that person contributes to society or not. Let's say we agree that we can afford to provide those in need with a loaf of bread and 500ml of mineral water a day. Here is how this can happen at point of sale: the system first checks if the buyer has enough money in his account, if not – checks if he is sick, elderly, a kid, a pregnant woman (any of the conditions set as qualifying for social assistance). If the buyer does not meet any of these criteria, the system checks if he can be issued a personal emergency loan. If his credit limit is maxed out, the system will then generate the quanta (have everyone pay for this poor person's bread and water) and complete the transaction. This algorithm, along with the Employer of Last Resort algorithm, should eliminate any beggars from the city streets.

Personal emergency loan
Assume a buyer is out of money, and does not meet any of the criteria for social assistance – old age, poor health, pregnancy, orphan, etc. The system could easily issue new quanta, in an amount limited via a formula very much like those used by credit card companies today, and issue a personal emergency loan to the buyer. Such loans should have very high repayment rates, as the Employer of Resort functionality can always provide employment opportunity for loan repayment. The personal emergency loan, while a form of assistance, is debt-based money.

Spirituality and yoga; healthcare; education
Priests and yoga instructors, doctors and educators can issue new money at the point of sale for their own services – subject to certain limitations of course. This will mean even the poorest members of society are entitled to a sermon/yoga practice, to a basic health care package and basic education. Using the platform, it is possible to confer the "Midas touch" (i.e. capability to issue money on the spot) to any profession – judges, public coaches, artists, etc, if this is what society wishes. The point here is if the provider of a given good/service is bestowed with the "Midas touch" – society will be encouraged to use that good/service, as even the poorest members of society will consume

it, courtesy of the more affluent members of society. For example: if coiffeurs can issue money at the point of purchase on the basis of need, chances are members of this society will go around with really nice hairdos, as even the poorest ones will be able to afford great hairstyling. Changing the composition – the source - of the money supply, has significant motivational effect on the members of society and allows the channeling of society's resources into commonly agreed upon activities. The Bitcoin is one such example.

Computer security on the Internet
Borrowing ideas from the Bitcoin, new money could be issued for those users who update daily their anti-virus defenses – this will both encourage significant investments into anti-virus software, and will motivate users to not let their machines be used in various malware attacks. Keeping the public transaction ledger – the blockchain – is another obvious prime candidate for money printing, as the Bitcoin has already clearly demonstrated.

Employer of Last Resort
The Employer of Last Resort functionality is fundamental within the quantum economy. It allows unlimited demand for human labor at 1Q/hour. If a certain activity is designated as "Employer of Last Resort-eligible", then those practicing it can be issued new money for doing it. There will always be funding for it. Such an activity must have the following characteristics: (1) it must be in the public benefit, (2) it must be able to be carried out by people without special training, (3) can utilize labor in relatively small chunks – 1 hour, for example. Let us consider two possible examples: community work and reforestation:

ELR: Community work, reforestation.
Say we bestow "Employer of Last Resort" functionality to community work – sweeping the streets, painting the public buildings, repairing the public benches, landscaping those public gardens. The community can elect its local "Employer of Last Resort", who will have the duty to constantly provide employment opportunities at 1Q/hour within his/her community. The inspiration for this program is drawn from the military "If it moves – salute it! If it doesn't – move it! If you can't – paint it!". Anyone with military experience will testify how work *never (!)* ends in the military – there is always something to clean, sweep, repair, repaint - an obvious example how human labor can always be applied to improve the environment, assuming absence of budgetary constraints.

Assuming broad penetration of Google Glass type of devices, it would be possible to have an ELR center with the government, 24/7, where anyone can call and via Google Glass stream evidence of useful public work done in her community – and get paid on the spot by confirmation of the ELR staff with newly issued money. Theoretically, it would be possible to pull your car by the road, call the ELR center, repair the road fences, paint the traffic signs – say for an hour or so – and earn 1Q. The same reasoning can be applied for reforestation.

The Employer of Last Resort functionality, if properly implemented, would mean an end to unemployment. Every member of the quantum society is entitled to 6 to 8 hours of productive effort at 1Q/hour. For higher pay - either put in more brawn, or more brains.

The Employer of Last Resort algorithm, along with the store of value defenses, gives value to the quant.

For social algorithms to work, all value accounts must reside within the system. The operation of social algorithms is incompatible with the operation of the current system of banking.

"The test of our progress is not whether we add more to the abundance of those who have much; it is whether we provide enough for those who have little"
F.D. Roosevelt

"How many have the talent to become a Steven Spielberg, a Jane Austen, or an Albert Einstein? We know there was at least one of each, and maybe one is all we're allotted. I cannot help but believe, though, that there are many talented people whose aspirations and potential have been thwarted by economics and their lack of tools....The Information highway will open undreamed-of artistic and scientific opportunities to a new generation of geniuses."
Bill Gates, "The Road Ahead"

The payment system and the digital personal wallet

In the quantum economy, a multitude of currencies are integrated into a unified monetary system under a common pattern and circulate simultaneously as media of exchange. All currencies are created using the same underlying pattern, but each issuer provides a currency with a different "flavor" within that unifying fundamental architecture.

Choice in currency within the quantum monetary realm is realized by allowing users to *filter* incoming payments. The filter sets minimum criteria that have to be met in order for a payment to be executed between the payee and the payer. A money market facilitates the exchange between currencies to ensure the execution of economic transactions between actors that do not have direct coincidence in their monetary preferences/filters.

Public space quanta are universally acceptable and *cannot be rejected* as a valid means of payment. You can do no wrong with public quanta – they are always 100% backed, their market value is always equal to face value, and are universally accepted. But they are the fastest ones to rust in your wallet – this is made to give an edge to the commercial quanta, which have risk imbedded into them, but keep their value longer. Large transactions will most likely be carried out in public quanta only – just like in the past, when gold was used for large transactions, whereas silver (commercial quanta) was preferred for retail payments.

Commercial quanta *can be rejected* for payment. Accepting a commercial quant indicates belief in the issuer of the quant, hence such quanta are likely to encourage the development of the local economy. By accepting somebody's commercial quanta the payee makes a very clear statement in her belief in the issuer's credibility and trustworthiness.

Finally, the payment system is completely isolated from any financial system risks. No one is "systemically important". No one is "too big to fail". The bitter medicine of capitalism's creative destruction can be applied to anyone, at any time.

The Quantum Money System: Summary

The Quantum Money System is a payment system. Nothing that Visa, MasterCard, etc. haven't already done. Only it is a payment system smarter than the existing ones – it knows details about the payment transaction which allow it to issue new money on the spot – if, when, where, and in amounts in accordance with the accepted social contract. It also knows the revenues of a business and allows businesses to issue their own obligations (money) on that basis, too. The money unit itself is multi-dimensional data structure with a labor-standard base. The information-rich environment allows the minimization of the discovery costs in a bank-independent Hayekian currency discovery process, which is the conceptual backbone of the system. The control over the amount of money in the economy is carried out by the Demurrage Bot, via a negative feedback loop with the Consumer Price Index. The system is designed to be self-regulating in the achievement of the society's monetary goals.

The key elements of business credit – working capital financing and long-term debt financing - are established within the proposed IT architecture. More complex financial instruments – equities trading, commodities contracts, derivatives of all sorts, etc. – can be implemented as a variety of software apps.

THE QUANTUM MONEY SYSTEM:

(1) DISINTERMEDIATES THE STATE AND THE FRACTIONAL-RESERVE BANKING SYSTEM FROM THE PRODUCTION OF MONEY

(2) SIGNIFICANTLY REDUCES GOVERNMENT'S INTERMEDIATION IN SOCIAL PROGRAMS

———————————

EXPECTED BENEFITS OF THE QUANTUM MONEY SYSTEM

1. *Separation of money from the state,* enhancing the power of the individual vis-à-vis the state, making wars, devaluations, deficits, inflation, periodic crises less likely.

2. *Elimination of inflation and stability of the currency unit without the use of a commodity anchor (gold, silver).* Courtesy of the Demurrage Bot and the peer pressure of the collective.

3. *Elimination of hunger.* No one needs to starve. A loaf of bread and a bottle of water a day can always be provided via newly printed money if the assistance recipient meets the qualification criteria.

4. *Elimination of unemployment.* Everyone is entitled to provide productive output to society via the Employer of Last Resort algorithms, allowing unlimited demand for labor at 1Q/hour.

5. *Elimination of poverty.* Through the Employer of Last Resort algorithms, through better access to education, healthcare and entrepreneurial financing.

6. *Reduction of inequality.* On the down side, extreme forms of poverty will be eliminated; on the up side, holders of liquid wealth will bear the largest burden of the social algorithms (via demurrage).

7. *Reduction in frequency and severity of boom-bust cycles (bubbles)*

8. *Increased funding for education, health care, and other public projects while simultaneously keeping government out of the money system and much of the social programs*

9. *Solution for the unfunded liabilities problem.* These will stop being a government's concern any more.

10. *Solution for the mounting debts problem.* Debt levels in society will be reduced across the board; governments will have smaller balance sheets, and better funding through the Quantum Bank.

11. *Alleviation of global warming.* Negative and positive externalities can be priced into the money system; abundant public funding will support "green" public projects.

12. *Small government and massive privatization.* Since everyone will have a basic income, massive privatizations are possible. Social security taxes, unemployment benefits taxes and health-related taxes will end. Taxation will be focused on consumption.

13. *Ease of access to capital for entrepreneurs*

14. *Return of the community.* Support of local businesses on a peer-to-peer basis, availability of money for local public works, work for everyone in small community projects and community upkeeping.

15. *Factor price equalization.* In the quantum currency union, the minimum wage across countries will be the same.

16. *Ease of formation of currency unions; end to trade wars.* The monetary problems currently faced by the European Union are largely avoided in the quantum currency union.

WHY THE QUANTUM MONEY SYSTEM

Technological evolution must go hand in hand with personal and societal evolution

Humanity is still learning to use the power given to it through technology. The horrors of World War II became possible on such a large scale precisely because there was the technology to enable it – the tank, the airplane, the submarine, the machine gun. Couple that technology with the fear-driven minds of leaders at the time – and the result is suffering on unimaginable scale. Currently, nuclear arsenals are supposedly kept under control through the Mutually Assured Destruction (MAD) doctrine. How applicable that doctrine will be 20 years from now when even small groups of people will have the technology for weapons of mass destruction? …Wonder why your grand-grand-grand parents did not participate in the Dutch tulip mania? Lack of connectivity. They didn't have cell phones and e-mail at the time, so they didn't *know* about the "great investment" in tulip bulbs and couldn't easily "wire" the money. Wonder how the whole world got into the subprime mortgage debacle – couple greed and competitiveness with a phone line and a payment system and – voila!

Obviously, it's not the phone line – it's the *greed* at the end of the phone line that did the trick. And now the bombs are getting bigger, the guns are 3D-printed at home, the communication lines stream in HD. The power of a person's mind – previously constrained by his own two hands and legs, and his voice – is being multiplied, via the steam engine and the search engine, *ad infinitum.*

> **"… THEY MAY LEAD US … TO THE BUDDHA OR TO THE BOMB, AND IT IS UP TO EACH OF US TO DECIDE WHICH ROAD TO TAKE[19]"**

Technology inexorably exacerbates the distance on that continuum – between the Buddha and the Bomb, allowing us to do ever greater good through technology, or inflict ever greater damage; and more and more puts that choice squarely with each one of us.

Maybe we need a new philosophy for the technologically advanced Information Age. A new set of personal, interpersonal and societal norms and values. Something different from the mechanistic, distributive, me-vs-you silo thinking of the Industrial Age. Something within the lines of Open vs. Closed, Transparent vs. Secret, Shared vs. Individually owned, Peer-to-Peer vs. Intermediated, Dynamic vs. Static, Adaptive vs. Rigid, Fluid vs. Structured, Self-and community-regulated vs. Government-controlled, Enough vs. More, Abundant vs. Scarce.

One thing is for sure, though - we can't have a society that's technologically advanced while being bitterly divided over nationality, race, religion, wealth; which is histrionically competitive, with disregard for values and environment; with large parts of the population marginalized, unemployed, disenfranchised – such a society will end badly, one way or another.

> **IN THE LONG RUN, FOCUSING ON TECHNOLOGY WITHOUT FOCUSING ON THE SELF MAY TURN OUT TO BE THE GREATEST TECHNOLOGY-RELATED RISK FOR SOCIETY AT LARGE.**

The Gods did not nail Prometheus to the rocks just for nothing, you know.

The Quantum Money System is, thus, first and foremost, a *social* technology - social technology designed to alleviate the distributive pressures within a technologically advanced, democratic, free market society. It brings *call-optionality* to the social contract: limited, hedged downside risk – freedom from hunger, poverty, unemployment, poor health, and lack of education - while providing unlimited upside potential for those having the vision, courage, execution skill and willingness to put in what it takes to succeed.

The great empires of the past – the Lydians', the Romans', the Greeks' - were built on plentiful slave labor and sound money. Technology is about to provide both in abundance – via robotics and software algorithms. If history is any guide, great prosperity should lie ahead – assuming we don't kill each other in the meantime over staggering debts, over diminishing resources, over nationalistic, religious or any other type of segregations.

---

[19] *Fritjof Capra "The turning point"*

THE BIGGER PROMISE OF IT: PUBLIC GOVERNANCE

Many scholars have examined the essential link between political freedom and economic freedom – Milton Freedman and his classic "Capitalism and Freedom", Hayek and "The Road to Serfdom", Henry C. Simons and "Economic Order for a Free Society", etc. – it is a long list. And when put to the test, societies with centrally planned economies (and the political regimes that come with central planning) eventually wither, while societies with decentralized economies and decentralized political power grow and prosper. Lately, however, capitalism and democracy seem to be, strangely enough, at odds with each other.

Lawrence Lessig, in his book "Republic, lost" talks about "how money corrupts Congress – and a plan to stop it":

- "The great threat today is instead in plain sight. It is an economy of influence now transparent to all, which has normalized a process that draws our democracy away from the will of the people."
- "We have created an engine of influence that seeks not some particular strand of political or economic ideology, whether Marx or Hayek. We have created instead an engine of influence that seeks simply to make those most connected rich."

Joseph Stiglitz, in his book "The Price of Inequality" uses the terms "a democracy in peril", and "one dollar one vote" to describe the political battleground between the average citizen and moneyed interests. Al Gore, in his book "The Future" says "Democracy and capitalism have been hacked. The results are palpably obvious in the suffocating control of policy decisions by the elites".

How could a political system based on individual freedom (democracy) and an economic system based on individual freedom (capitalism) be at odds with each other? The short answer is: Money. Not "money" as in "bribes", or some dark conspiracy theory cast on the American people by the devious "1%" - no. The currently observed threats to democracy are only logical consequences of the money system currently in use: ever-increasing inequality is virtually assured through the "preferential attachment" feature of the interest-charged money system, the built-in growth requirement via interest means ever larger businesses must compete ever more ferociously – they have bills to pay, they have competitors - domestic and international, there are dwindling natural resources. Naturally, Congress comes under ever increasing pressure from ever-larger businesses, with election campaigns logically getting ever more expensive, and lobbying efforts becoming ever more well-heeled and intense. The "average American" gets stomped out. This is a *monetary issue*, this is *money* casting its long shadow over other social systems and arrangements – at least *money* in its current form. It's not *democracy per se*, and not *capitalism per se* (as many a misguided protester may think) that are to blame. It's *money*. But *money* is ever so subtle, so invisible, like the water in that proverbial fish tank, and we are so used to it that very few of us ever take a deep hard look into it.

Way more pernicious to democracy, however, is the ever-increasing severity and scope of recurrent financial crises, predicated via the current monetary and financial architectures operating in an increasingly interconnected world. Right now, after the 2007/2008 crisis forced the use of every piece of financial ammunition in the US, both the Federal Reserve chairwoman and the President are out of bullets – and the only bullets left are those in the gun chambers. Yet another crisis of the 2007/2008 variety, given the amount of existing government debt and the amount of dollars already in circulation will most likely mean that Americans in uniforms will have to stand against Americans in jeans – without a clear resolution in sight. Let us remind you there was a time when America was supposed to be the land of the free. The Founding Fathers may soon be turning in their graves.

The purpose of this book is to communicate the message that there may be another bullet – and not just any bullet, but one of the proverbial "silver" variety. But it is not a bullet designed to be fired by Presidents – it will misfire in the hands of government; and it is not a bullet designed to be fired by the Federal Reserve – if anything, it is designed to end the Fed. It is a bullet buried in the Silicon Valley.

IT can help a democracy under fire from *money* in two ways - through alternative money systems and direct democracy:

Alternative money systems.

At least one information-based money system – the Quantum Money System introduced in this book – can alleviate the currently existing distributive pressures in society, allowing for full employment, better access to education, health care and social security; it can greatly reduce inequality by penalizing most heavily the "idle rich" – those not using accumulated resources for productive purposes; it can eliminate the risks for the payment system and the new money creation system - risks currently emanating from "too big to fail" institutions having mismanaged a variety of financial system and operating risks – thus providing stable monetary and hence economic environment; and it can also provide both entrepreneurs and the public sector with abundant funding. Using large, integrated IT platforms, new money systems of virtually every variety, strand, shape, form, and size, designed for every taste and preference – can be put forward; in the Information Age, banking is not – not by far! – the only possible way to organize the medium of exchange, store of value, unit of account functions within society; far better-performing money systems can be tailor-made to specifically address social issues, using information as the backbone of the money system. In the Information Age,

---

Banking is a legacy system

Direct democracy.

Through IT, every citizen can have *legislative initiative*, in a Wiki format. New laws can be put forward and designed through the power of collective intelligence – easily - with only modest expert oversight.

Strong, secure biometric identification and encryption technologies can enable *anonymous voting on anything* from our likes of the latest Dolce & Gabbana shoes to the proposed new laws or the job done by any publicly elected official – at virtually no cost. Elections and referenda can be held at any time, on any issue.

IT can also provide *transparency over the executive branch* of the state – just think what Google glass can do in this respect. If they (the government) can spy on us, we can "spy" on them.

Gradually, over the last two centuries, the composition and functioning of Congress have become hostage to moneyed interests. Allegiance to political parties occasionally seems to overcome allegiance to the country - despite the prescient warnings of George Washington on the dangers of political parties. In a technologically advanced society where everyone can vote easily on virtually anything at zero cost, intermediation via elected officials is a *limitation on the voting rights of the citizens*. In the Information Age,

---

Congress is a legacy system

Another name for the replacement of one form of public governance with another is *"revolution"*. This one may come, however, through firing bits, not bullets.

It is possible to (1) code the social contract into a smart, distributed money supply system, largely (1.1) disintermediating the banking system from the money supply, and (1.2) disintermediating the IRS, and the government in general from active management of most social programs.

It is possible to (1) create and pass laws, (2) control government, and (3) hold referenda on virtually anything at virtually anytime and anyplace – largely disintermediating Congress from the democratic process - using IT.

These things are not like gravity, you know – they were made by man, they can be changed by man.

"How quickly can institutions be adapted to the Internet?....long established institutions are notoriously resistant to change. The speed with which business models have been disintermediated and new models have emerged offers reason for hope"
                                                                                    Al Gore, "The Future"

SUMMARY

There are three fundamental societal liberties - rights of participation in society - necessitated by the conjecture that collective intelligence, properly organized, in the long run produces better outcomes for the community than individual intelligence:

- Democracy - the power of collective intelligence brought to the governance of the commons.
- Free Market (capitalism) - the power of collective intelligence brought to the creation of goods and services.
- Distributed Money System - the power of collective intelligence brought to the governance of money.

Too much restriction (centralization) in any one of these liberties can destroy the other two.

Information technology can be used as a tool to either enhance, or to limit, these liberties.

Money, in particular, is not the neutral measuring rod often assumed in economics. *Money* can have a variety of architectures, each architecture with its specific effects on society.

The money system currently in use has the following fundamental flaws, which are becoming more pronounced with the passage of time and with the advancement of the networked society:

- The money system is top-heavy, centralized.
- Money is issued as debt only, against interest, for narrowly defined (and narrowly shared) profit.
- Both the payment system and the issuance of new money are vulnerable to mismanagement of credit risk and maturity transformations by inherently unstable, fractional-reserve based banking system.
- The stability of the store of value function of money is not assured.

This results in instability of the economic system, as described by Hyman Minsky, hence the necessity for top-down intervention that came to be known as Keynesianism. The scope of Keynesianism is limited, though, as its long run consequences are unsustainable level of government debt and depreciating fiat currency.

Other negative consequences of the current money system are negative externalities (most notably climate change), currency and trade wars, inequality, unemployment, growth imperative, hyper-competitiveness, resource depletion.

A change of the money system is a very fundamental change that society as a whole can undertake, and given the current tools society has – a very difficult and uncertain one.

It is possible to devise an infinite number of money systems based on information technology - as global public goods to be used voluntarily by communities of various sizes – from as few as two people to all of humanity. This book proposes a concept for the creation of one such public good – the Quantum Money System.

The Quantum Money System is a bank-independent money system that seeks to eliminate hunger, poverty, unemployment, to encourage greater access to education, health care, and economic opportunity, to reduce the frequency and severity of financial market crises, to largely eliminate instability within the economy, to reduce the inequality gap (or at least to limit it on the downside), to alleviate global warming, to promote democracy.

The proposed concept is only at its earliest stages of development, and its successful completion and practical implementation is far from certain. It will take very large amounts of time, effort, resources, and leadership.

AFTERWORD

*You've read the magic words. You've breathed the air. The change is irreversible. You've been **infected** – infected with the virus of distributed money supply. You are about to experience the following disturbing side effects:*

- *You'll be driving home from work, and looking at all the dirt vehicles bring onto the streets, and all the leaves falling from trees – and you will be seeing **money**…And you will realize that once again America can be the country it used to be generations ago for our forefathers as they were arriving into the land of milk and honey – a land where the streets are paved with gold and money grows on trees, only this time the beacon of hope is not in the hand of the Statute of Liberty, but in the Googles, the Apples, and the Facebooks of the world;*
- *As you drive on, you will see a group of protesters, protesting against something - inequality, unemployment, capitalism – and you will think "What if all those people could get work right there and then, from as little as one hour to a whole lifetime? Any amount of work they needed? As a guaranteed right of every member of society?"*
- *And you will pass by a bum going through the garbage bins, and will think "What if we lived in a society where no one needed to go through the garbage bins – for food or basic necessities?"*
- *And then you will be listening on the car radio, about the government's staggering debts, the unfunded liabilities, and you will think "What if instead you could listen to a message that the Quantum Bank is flush with cash, cash for public projects? And the government was so very small…And it had nothing to do with people's pensions - fully funded at any time as long as businesses provided goods and services?";*
- *And then you will be driving by a decrepit public school, and you will be thinking "What if there were no public schools? What if all schools were private? If the government was only the standard setter for the education industry – an industry as exciting and fun as Disney? But every student – even those from the poorest families – had the money to choose the right teacher/school for him?"*
- *And you will be listening on the radio of yet another failed government health care program – the latest in a long string of failed government health care programs – and you will be thinking "What if all the government had to do for health was to make sure the hospitals are clean and the drugs are safe – and everything else was private? Yet each one of us, even the poorest – had the money for basic health care?"*

The list goes on and on and on…You got the idea.

*Is this project doable? It's too early to tell. But if you dare dream – dream that a project like this **is** doable – then next time you drive your car in the middle of nowhere and see one of those Google Internet balloons hovering up in the air, you will know something way bigger than just free e-mail and Youtube videos – you'll know no one around goes hungry, and no one goes unemployed.*

We leave you here, with a shared dream. And the strangest of questions – if this dream is technologically possible, how come it's just a dream?